HUNTING IN ALASKA AND FISHING

By Dr. Duane R. Lund

Lund S&R Publications

Distributed By:
Adventure Publications
820 Cleveland • Cambridge, MN 55008

ISBN-10: 0-9740821-4-7
ISBN-13: 978-0-9740821-4-1

DEDICATION

To Lloyd and Barb Olson of Anchorage, Alaska. Not only have they been very special, life-long friends, but without their invitation and encouragement I would never have enjoyed all these years of hunting and fishing in this great state.

PART ONE
HUNTING IN ALASKA

PART II
FISHING IN ALASKA

PART I
HUNTING IN ALASKA

Little did I know that I was flying with a bush pilot legend – Babe Alsworth.* As we flew over the Alaskan tundra in the old Taylorcraft pontoon plane looking for caribou, the pilot leaned over and asked if I had a strong stomach. I assured him that I did, and at which time he turned the plane in a slightly different direction and pointed to a brown bear with three cubs ambling across the tundra. Suddenly, he lowered the aircraft and began circling the bears in smaller and smaller circles. The mother bear came to a stop, all the while looking up at the airplane as it drew closer and closer until it seemed to me that the animals were just off our wing tip. Suddenly it rose up on its hind legs and began pawing the air in our direction. "There," Babe said, "That's what I wanted you to see!"

All of this was happening on my third day in Alaska. It was already well worth my trip from Minnesota.

When my friends, Lloyd and Barb Olson, moved to Anchorage a few months earlier, they insisted that I come up for a visit. Because they were good friends I wanted to accept their invitation, but when Lloyd called to say that if I came in early fall we would go hunting, I ordered my plane ticket! Before the end of our telephone conversation he went on to say that some members of his and Barb's church were about to start a guiding and outfitting business on Lake Iliamna, (the biggest lake in Alaska) about a two hour flight in a small plane from Anchorage. It turned out we were to be their first customers.

We could have flown to Iliamna in a commercial plane, but Paul Carlson, our guide to be, advised chartering a small plane because it would take us through Lake Clark Pass, which he promised would be a spectacular experience. He was so right. For nearly an hour of that flight we had mountains and glaciers off one or both wing tips. It was a rather rough flight but well worth the discomfort.

When we arrived at the Iliamna airport we were met by our hosts: Paul and Irene Carlson, Jack and Lynn Vantrease and Chuck and Barb Crapechetts. (Irene and Chuck were both teachers in the Eskimo village, which was called "Iliamna").

---

*Babe Alsworth moved to Alaska in the 1930s and earned a living as a bush pilot for the next half century, but in the process founded the community of Port Alsworth on Lake Clark and ran a fairly large farm where he grew radishes more than a food long and enormous heads of cabbage. He flew scores of prospectors but liked to be paid in gold dust or nuggets rather than cash. In spite of all the hazards of flying in Alaska, he was over ninety years of age when he died of natural causes.

The rack from my first caribou as displayed in my cabin on the Lake of the Woods, Ontario.

Paul had arranged for Babe Alsworth to pick us up the next morning. Since his Taylorcraft was a small plane, he would need to make two trips to ferry Paul, Lloyd and me to a hunting site. Paul had asked Babe to pick out a site near any place where we saw caribou grazing and we were looking for such a place when Babe spotted the four bears.

I was Babe's only passenger this first trip – along with all our camping equipment. Shortly after harassing the bears, we began to see scattered small herds of caribou. Babe chose a small lake for our campsite. As we coasted into shore, Babe observed, "That herd of caribou is working this way and they will probably pass between this lake and that smaller lake up the shore. You can run up the shore and stay hidden behind that ridge that follows the shoreline and you may be in range when they pass between the two lakes." (In those days you could hunt the same day you fly.)

I nodded my agreement and as we touched shore I got out of the plane and loaded my 30-06. Babe cautioned, "You'll have to hurry, they're moving pretty fast."

Bending over to stay hidden behind the ridge that formed the shoreline, I ran as fast as I could. Finally, out of wind after running nearly a mile, I rested on one knee while trying to catch my breath. Suddenly, while I was still down on one knee, the tips of several antlers appeared above the ridge, about 30 yards away! Slowly I raised up and there they were, the whole herd of seventeen caribou, less than 40 yards away! I picked out the largest bull – which really wasn't all that big but I was used to white tail antlers and I thought this caribou might be a record. The animal was walking broadside to me and I had plenty of time to take aim behind the front shoulder and fired just once. The caribou was obviously well hit but I made the mistake of letting him stagger to the shore of the smaller lake – really a pond – and there he went down for keeps.

I looked back and saw Babe coming up the shore so I just stayed put. When he arrived he shook my hand and said, "Now I'll butcher the animal and take it back to Iliamna as I pick up Lloyd and Paul."

When I asked how I could help he replied with a smile, "Just stay out of my way."

To my amazement, Babe took out a pocket jackknife and proceeded to butcher the bull into four quarters, the back straps and two neck roasts. In those days we could leave the rib cage. It was all done in a matter of minutes. He then observed, "I think I can land and take off from this pond."

First, we unloaded the camping gear on the shore of the lake and then he took off and landed the pontoon plane on the pond. I helped him load the meat, but before he took off, Babe observed, "I don't like the looks of the sky back towards Iliamna. It's just possible I won't be able to return with the other guys (and they had all the food) until tomorrow. But you'll be all right. You have the tent and your sleeping bag and you can always cook caribou meat off the rib cage – and I'll leave you some pilot bread."

Babe handed me a can of what looked like huge soda crackers.

Our first camp, nothing fancy!

The autumn tundra has all the color of a Minnesota hardwood forest. This is the pond from which Babe Alsworth took off in his float plane.

Our guide, Paul Carlson, butchering Lloyd's cow.

I asked what I should do If he couldn't come back tomorrow. He replied, "Just stay put; there is no way you can walk out of here. There are three rivers between here and Iliamna."

His parting words were, "Be sure you watch my take-off." And watch I did as Babe began circling the pond at a faster and faster clip until he knew he had enough speed to lift off the pond. His pontoons seemed inches above the flat tundra but since there were no tall trees that was enough height. With a dip of his wings he was off to Iliamna.

As I sat there watching the plane become nothing more than a dot on the horizon I suddenly felt very much alone, more alone than I had ever felt in my life.

My mind drifted back to the four bears – where were they now? They were only about two miles away when we landed. And then I began to worry about the weather. Then I began to wonder about the tent; I hadn't set one up since my days in Boy Scouts. I had too much on my mind to enjoy the beauty of the tundra and the mountains – mountains far higher than I had seen in my lifetime. Then, in what seemed an amazingly short time, I heard an airplane, and then I saw it – Babe was coming back – I was saved from a night of loneliness!

By the time we had unloaded the plane and set up the tent, it was time for supper. Paul's wife, Irene, had at one time taught Home Economics in the Grand Marais High School, in Minnesota, and she demonstrated her skills by pre-cooking our lunches and dinners. Strange after all these years that I can still recall that first supper – she called it "Russian Reunion". It was a sort of boiled dinner featuring canned sockeye salmon. That recipe along with several others of Irene's creations have found their way into a couple of my cookbooks, including this one. Paul was a lousy cook, and Irene knew it, so she prepared meals that only had to be heated. In the years that have followed, I have taken over the cooking chores from Paul.

After dinner, Paul created a campfire from driftwood and dead alder brush. As darkness set in we were treated to the most spectacular display of northern lights I had ever seen. There were hues of red and green never seen in Minnesota. This show plus the campfire loosened our tongues, and as we visited into the night, bonds of friendship formed that have lasted our three lifetimes.

When I awoke in the morning, I became aware of the fact that only my head and shoulders were inside the tent. The rest of my body, in my sleeping bag, had slid outside the tent. Paul had chosen a site with a slant so that in case of rain, the water would run underneath the plastic sheet we had for a floor. If that bear had come along it could easily have pulled me the rest of the way out! I did notice, however, that Paul (and only Paul for safety reasons) slept with a loaded rifle – just in case.

After a breakfast of bacon and eggs that even Paul couldn't ruin, Lloyd and I began our hunt. In those days we could each buy three caribou licenses (at only $25 each); we each had purchased two. We chose hills about a mile apart and spent the morning enjoying nice weather and the scenery but seeing nothing. The afternoon was much the same but then, shortly before dark, I saw Lloyd stand up, put down his rifle, and extended his arms upward so that he looked remarkably like a caribou. Then he seemed to be pointing at me. I stood up, and there at the bottom of my hill was a nice caribou bull which was about to pass by me unnoticed. A single shot from the 30-06 again did the job. Having heard the shot, Paul arrived shortly thereafter and then, like Babe, butchered the animal in a matter of minutes. It took another year of hunting before I could use a knife to separate the quarters from the rest of the body and likewise disjoint the hams and the knees and then cut out the neck roasts and backstraps. The hide was left on the quarters to keep them clean and to keep off blow-flies.

Babe was due back the afternoon of the third day, so Lloyd and I returned to the hunt anxious to at least get him a shot. Shortly after leaving camp we saw a loan caribou grazing about a half-mile away. We concealed ourselves down wind, behind a small ridge and waited and waited. It was getting close to noon and we knew we were running out of time before Babe's arrival. I volunteered to make a wide circle around the caribou and let her smell me (it was a cow). When I was bout a half-mile on the other side of the animal it smelled me. I must have smelled pretty bad after three days without a shower because it suddenly pointed its nose in the air, got a good whiff, and took off running at full speed right towards Lloyd - who waited until he was nearly run over before putting the animal down.

Lloyd and I agreed that this caribou hunting was pretty easy, but we would learn over the years that it wasn't always that simple.

After our return to the lodge on Lake Iliamna, Lloyd and I enjoyed a couple of days of trout fishing on the Newhalen River (which joins Lake Clark and Lake Iliamna) before returning to Anchorage on a commercial flight. Our favorite spot was below the falls near the airport. Our take was rainbow, Dolly Varden* and grayling.

CARIBOU BASICS

After twenty-five years of hunting Alaskan caribou, a guy should be an expert, but as in all kinds of hunting, you never know it all and I only feel comfortable sharing some of the basics.

I would begin by saying that caribou are surely among the most enjoyable animals to hunt. Perhaps most important for me is where they are hunted. For those of us who love the out of doors, the beauty and magnificence of the environment make it all worthwhile even if we never fired a shot. Nowhere in the world are the mountains more spectacular and the tundra has a beauty all its own — especially in the fall of the year when the tiny berry bushes take on all the color of a hardwood forest.

---

* The Dolly Varden is actually a char and gets its name from Miss Dolly Varden, a character in Charles Dickens' classic, "Barnaby Ridge", who wore a pink polka-dot dress.

The caribou themselves are worthy trophies. Even the cows have antlers — although not as spectacular as the bulls. They are large animals. Even a calf in the fall of the year is the size of a typical whitetail doe. Bulls can go over 500 pounds. The meat is excellent. I can best describe it as something between a deer and an elk. And I have never had tough caribou meat. Because the meat is so lean, it is a very healthful food. All of the fat is carried on their backs, not the meat. The caribou is unique in that each hair contains air cells, so much air that when they swim their backs are visible above the surface of the water.

There are two kinds of caribou: barren ground and woodland. Where we have hunted in Alaska they are the barren variety. The descriptors, of course, describe their habitat. Woodland caribou don't migrate as much.

What are the downsides of hunting caribou? What about mosquitoes? I'm sure mosquitoes are a problem in many parts of Alaska, but they have never been a problem for us. However, gnats (or "white socks" as many Alaskans call them) can be worse than mosquitoes because the itchy little hives that result from a bite will probably bother you all through the hunt and you may even take the itching home with you. the good news is that they don't like wind, and Alaska is often windy, and they are not a problem after dark. If you keep your skin covered they are not a problem, but insect repellents are not very helpful. The gnats have never been so bad that I have had to wear netting over my head.

Now, let's talk hunting. In my experience, the caribou is not as wary as deer, but as described in the opening story, once they smell you they are long gone! I have been told that natives can carry a branch of alder brush (to resemble antlers) on their shoulders and then walk slouched over, against the wind, until they are in range of caribou. All I know is that has never worked for us.

Alaskan caribou seem to be always on the move. I have heard it said that caribou can walk up to eight miles an hour and still be able to snatch a mouthful of tundra here and there while on the move. It is very possible to sneak on a resting herd (we've done it many times) but, it is almost impossible to catch up with a herd that is on the move. One legend is that an Eskimo's idea of Hell is being destined to be very hungry and always in sight of caribou but the herd is always disappearing over the next ridge almost immediately after they come in sight! I have experienced Eskimo Hell many times!

Most of us from "the lower forty-eight" have seen movies of huge herds of caribou migrating. This does happen in many parts of alaska as the animals move to and from winter feeding grounds or to and from calving grounds. All of our experiences have been on the Alaskan Peninsula, where the caribou spend their summers on the high hills and mountains away from the gnats and other insects and then, as snow comes to the higher elevations, move down onto the tundra as summer ends and cold nights and increasing winds take care of the bug problems. The barren caribou are, in deed, usually on the move but not on treks many miles long. The largest herds I have seen would be well under 100. Many times caribou, especially bulls, will be alone. The typical herd, in our experience would be half a dozen to twenty in number.

Because caribou are so often on the move, one of the best and easiest ways to hunt them is to pick a fairly high spot where there is good visibility in all directions and grass or brush tall enough to conceal you , and just wait. Sometimes, when you see where the animals are headed, you can get there first. Other times, patience will be rewarded as they come to you. It is important to choose a campsite where fairly large numbers of caribou can be seen from the air. In our experience, our guide or pilot knew where the caribou were and picked a campsite accordingly. Only once, in all these years, did we have to move.

We usually were flown in by pontoon plane and therefore set up camp on a lake – and lakes are everywhere. As a Minnesotan, I have been proud of our 14,000 lakes, but Alaska has well over 100,000! Because packing caribou meat is never easy, it is a

Chad Longbella packing the meat from one half of his caribou. If the meat had been packed higher on his shoulders, Chad would have had an easier carry.

good idea to hunt and shoot animals fairly close to water where the airplane can pick up the meat. However, with a good packboard with the meat riding high on your shoulders, it isn't that difficult to carry out up to a half an animal at a time. For a long haul, the meat can be de-boned and skinned to reduce weight. (May no longer be legal everywhere.)

Because the tundra looks so flat and because you can see for miles it is deceiving. The natives have a legend that caribou can disappear into the ground and then reappear out of the ground. This has been my experience so many times. Actually, there are scores of creek beds, some of them dry, that over the years have eaten into the tundra so that the caribou are down, out of sight. Many times I have watched caribou for hours, only to have them disappear never to be seen again. On the other hand, like the second caribou in the opening story, they can appear in range from nowhere. In one such instance, Rus Norberg and I had been watching a small group of caribou down in the valley, we were lying on a hill and out of range. They were feeding and constantly moving around. Suddenly they were gone. About that time I felt Rus' sharp elbow in my side as he whispered, "They're behind us!" They were so close that we had plenty of time to get up out of our awkward positions and each claim a nice animal.

I spoke earlier about sneaking on caribou. If the caribou are resting or just milling around as they graze, it is very possible and rewarding. The challenge is to stay down wind and find things to hide behind as you walk or crawl across the flat tundra. Fortunately, it is not as difficult as it sounds. There are hills and ridges across the tundra and creek beds, especially dry ones, that provide good cover.

One experience is especially memorable for me because it turned an empty-handed trip into filled licenses. It was one of those years when the warm weather hung on until well into autumn and the caribou simply did not come down from the mountains. The problem was exacerbated by the fact that the pilot who was suppose to fly us got drunk and was in no condition to fly. No other pilot was available, so Paul suggested we take a couple of pretty good size, outboard driven commercial fishing boats and go up the shore of Lake Iliamna about 30 miles to a place about as near the mountains as we could get by water. For four days we spread out looking for caribou but saw none. On the fifth and last day of the hunt, Don Hester, a frequent hunting and fishing partner from home, and I explored together. About mid-day, Don spotted a small herd of caribou through his binoculars; they appeared to be resting. Because of the lack of consistent cover, we probably walked and crawled two miles to cover the one mile between us and the animals. When we were finally in a long range, at least 150 yards, a deep gully separated us from the caribou. There was no way we could sneak any closer without being seen. All of the animals (about a dozen) were lying down except for two, a bull and a cow that seemed to be on watch. There was such a strong wind in our faces that I probably could have spoken out loud, but I whispered to Don, "You saw them first; you shoot first. Which one do you want?"

Don whispered back, "That big bull on the right, lying down."

Don's rifle cracked and the bull never moved. I then took the standing bull and he went down with the first shot. In the excitement and confusion that followed, I'm not quite sure just what all happened, but Don and I both shot automatics and other members of our party who could hear us said it sounded like war. The herd, of course, took off at full gallop. I do remember hearing Don count, "Two down…that's three…number four…and five! Stop shooting!"

When we finally climbed the far side of the ravine and reached our animals, we found four very nice caribou and one calf. Don and I have argued for years as to who shot the calf.

Don Hester's bull caribou.

In contrast to all that work and frustration they sometimes do come easy. I recall one trip on the first day of the hunt when two of us were left in camp washing breakfast dishes and straightening up the inside of the tent. The chores finished, I started to leave the tent but was shocked to see a half dozen caribou trotting along well within range. My partner and I finally managed to fumble some shells into our rifles. My partner, Don, was to my left and he muttered, "Shoot right – I'll shoot left."

Don's bull went down almost immediately; mine stumbled, fell, then got up again. It took another shot to bring him down for keeps. As we were surveying our trophies, Don asked, "So where did you hit him the first time?"

Look as we might we only found the one hit behind the front shoulder. I finally spotted the second – it had gone through one of the antlers! I had heard that such a shot could knock an animal out; I guess it is true.

Speaking of shots from tents, my young doctor friend, Chris, on his first Alaskan hunt had been hunting a couple of days without an opportunity to even shoot. We had decided to hunt together that day and were nearly out of sight of camp when Chris discovered he had forgotten his binoculars. I sat down to wait for him. Then, while he was in the tent a respectable bull came walking over the hill behind the tent. I was too far away to yell, but as he left the tent he happened to glance back and saw the caribou. It was a long shot, but Chris flattened out on the ground. He got the animal in a single shot, but he also got scoped!

Although much of the shooting is long range, opportunities do occur at very close range. Early one morning I took a stand behind a huge rock on the edge of a ravine that led from a high hill down to the lake where we were camped. A heavy fog suddenly moved in and I couldn't see more that a hundred feet. Then, coming down the hill into my little ravine came a small herd. I never realized until then how fog can magnify objects. I was absolutely certain, at first, that they were moose. But it turned out they were caribou. The light breeze was blowing in my face so they could not smell me. They passed by me so close I could have shot from the hip! But I didn't, I played it safe.

Again, in contrast, I shall always remember my longest shot, 505 paces, and I take big steps. After a few years of hunting in Alaska I changed from my 30-06 automatic deer rifle to a .300 magnum Winchester, not because of distance shooting, but because we had just enough brushes with bears to make me concerned, and for that reason I chose bolt action.

This particular day I had intentionally spooked a fairly large herd of grazing caribou toward my partner, Don. I just circled way around them and let them smell me. This was the first day of that hunt and we had agreed that if the plan worked, he would only take one animal and let me shoot my own later. I watched from a distance as I saw a bull fall and then heard Don's shot. But to my surprise, fourteen or fifteen animals turned when he shot and started in my direction. As I have said, they were a very long way off, and, I should add, it was a very windy day. As they passed about as close as they were going to get I decided to give it a try. The animals were grouped very close together and I truly "flock-shot", leading and/or holding on various targets. I reloaded once. On my ninth shot, I quit. A respectable bull began to fall behind the herd and then fell. As I said, it took 505 paces to bring me to the area where I was shooting. I surely don't recommend this practice; there is too great a chance of just wounding an animal. But I will confess, it remains a good memory.

Changing the subject, long range shooting reminds me of how important it is to sight in your scope before you hunt. That lesson really hit home on a trip that included a dentist friend, Bob Mayhew. We were just flying into our camp site when Bob poked me and pointed out the window towards the ground. He had spotted a small herd of caribou; some grazing and others resting, along side a small lake. We touched down shortly thereafter on a larger lake about a mile from the caribou sighting.

After unloading the plane, I suggested to Bob that we try a sneak on the caribou. He was all for it. I talked our other hunters into setting up camp and the two of us took off. There was plenty of cover – mostly alder brush and willows and we didn't even have to do any crawling. I had mentioned to Bob that since he had spotted the caribou he was entitled to the first shot at an animal of his choice. When we were in easy range I nodded and Bob fired. I was quite surprised at his choice, because it was a cow that humped and then began running in a tight circle. I fired at a respectable bull Bob had passed on. I was pretty sure my first shot was lethal but the animal kept going so I fired twice more before it fell. Meanwhile, Bob emptied his rifle but with no apparent effect; the cow continued to run in a tight circle. I looked at Bob as he looked at me and said in frustration, "You'd better finish it off. Something must be wrong with my rifle. That isn't even the one I aimed at!"

I did as Bob requested. After making sure both animals were dead, Bob began to examine his gun and then said, "Look at my scope; you can see it is off with your naked eye! And i sighted it in before we left home!"

Sure enough, something had given the scope a hard hit between then and our arrival at the camp site. It was a good lesson for all of us, but as you will see in our chapter on moose hunting, it was a lesson forgotten by me.

In my experience, when packing for an Alaskan hunting or fishing trip, it is important to just assume there will be days with rain – sometimes very heavy rain. If you are going to be in tents on the tundra, take special precaution to keep your sleeping bag dry and to have rain gear that will keep you completely dry as you hunt. Because of the many creeks and streams, hip boots are also a must. If you plan to be out all day or hunt quite a ways from camp, just assume it may rain and dress accordingly.

On most of our trips, if wind with heavy rain came early in the trip, we would just stay in the tent all day and tell "war stories" rather than fight the elements. But if it was near the end of the trip and we still needed animals, we did venture out – or at least those of us who hadn't scored did.

I remember one such trip when we had experienced several days of awful weather, and it was a trip in which I hadn't even had a shot. I announced during breakfast that I was going to give it a try. No one volunteered to accompany me. Three of the guys had their animals and my friend, Don, who had shot many caribou over the years said, "Shoot one for me if you get a chance; otherwise I'll give it one more try in the morning." Which would be our last day. Weather permitting the plane would pick us up in the afternoon.

Animals, like humans, will seek shelter in bad weather so the hunter does have a pretty good idea of where to look for animals.

Sheltered from the prevailing winds.

The bull I shot in the rain now graces the top of the stairwell leading to my bedroom. Note the double shovels. In some parts of Alaska double shovels are extremely rare, but in the Iliamna area I would guess one in twenty bulls have them.

We were camped in a valley, probably pretty close to sea level. In back of us was a very high hill, almost a mountain, but not high enough to have snow. I knew that on the other side of that hill was a cliff and I was pretty sure it would be out of the wind at the bottom of that cliff. It turned out that the long climb up the hill was well worthwhile. As I had expected, and hoped, a pretty good size herd of caribou (about 30) were grazing or resting out of the driving rain. The countryside was pretty open so it demanded a long sneak, mostly on my hands and knees. When I was about 150 yards away, I sighted on a nice bull. Fortunately, the one shot was all I needed as the animal collapsed right where it was feeding. I say "fortunately" because the other caribou didn't seem to know where the shot came from and did not know which way to run. In retrospect, I think the sound bounced off the wall of the cliff which made it sound as though it came from behind them. Shooting at running animals at that distance would have been a real challenge, but I was able to select another nice standing bull for Don. It didn't fall on the first shot but took off running. I shot twice more before it dropped, but I only found one hole. I suspect I hit it that first standing shot but it just didn't go down right away.

I dressed out both animals but decided not to pack any meat back to camp, having to walk all the way into a heavy driving rain. I was confident the guys would help me pack it out in the morning – and they did.

When I reached the top of the hill and looked down into the valley where we were camped, I realized that if one of the tents hadn't been a florescent green I would not have been able to see where to go, that's how hard it was raining and blowing. The shortest route lead through patches of waist-high alders, but I was hesitant to go through the brushy areas for fear of flushing a bear that might be resting in their shelter. I knew the odds of that happening were small but I had been told that if you talked or sang you wouldn't surprise them and thereby would lessen the chance of an attack. So I took the shortcut through the brushy areas singing all the while, but not just singing any old songs, I sang hymns! And I didn't see any bears.

Of course there have been many other times we hunted in the rain. When three of our party, Greg Pappenfus and brothers Francis and Don Zetah, left camp that particular morning the sun was shining brightly and there was no sign of rain, but the men did wear rain gear, including hip boots. They walked a very long way that day and since it was the first day of hunting were careful to establish landmarks, or at least, so they thought. To make a very long story short, they eventually sighted a small herd that included three nice animals. The caribou were on the move, however, and it took most of the day to get in range. Fortunately, they were near a small lake where a plane could pick up the meat, or, they said they would not have shot. But shoot they did and killed three respectable bulls. By the time they butchered the meat and hauled it down to the shore of the lake, the weather made a dramatic change and soon it was pouring down rain. As they headed back towards camp, some of the landmarks were no longer visible. This was before the days of the GPS but they did have their compasses. That morning they had waded across two creeks, but when they encountered them on their return the heavy rain had flooded the streams where they had crossed before. They were forced in each case to walk a mile or two upstream so they could cross. Meanwhile it got dark. With the help of the compass they knew they were headed at least approximately in the right direction. they fired a rifle shot occasionally hoping that we would hear them back at camp and reply. The wind was strong, however, and in their faces, so we could not hear their shots back in camp, especially inside the tent. One of our crew remembered that if you turned up our Coleman cooking stove to wide open, the flame would shoot up more than a foot. So we filled the quart tank with gas and set the stove on a crate outside the tent at full force. One of our guys, Sherm Mandt, volunteered to stay up and tend the "torch" if necessary; the rest of us went to sleep but were gladly awakened by the hunters' return about midnight. they said they would never have found camp without the light from the stove. The rest of the story is that the next day our pilot stopped by but announced he could not land and take off on the little lake where they had left the meat. So the three hunters had to pack the meat to a larger lake – which lead them right past the spot where they had shot the caribou!

Speaking of packing meat, there are a lot of lessons to be learned. On one of our early trips, Lloyd Olson and I on the first day of hunting knew we had wandered a long way from camp, uphill all the way, but rationalized that if we shot something we would be carrying the meat downhill to camp. Lloyd spotted a single bull, a nice one, grazing in a place where it would be easy sneaking. By the time we were in range, the animal had laid down and Lloyd shot him in his bed. As we were butchering the animal, I just happened to glance up and there was a nice cow watching us from the hill we had snuck behind. Dry cows (those without calves) tend to be tender and excellent eating, so I had no hesitation in picking up my rifle and taking a shot. It dropped where it stood.

After butchering the second animal into quarters, back straps and shoulder roasts, we strapped half of each caribou to a back board and began our trek back to camp, all two miles of it. It was then that we learned going downhill, especially a steep hill, is more difficult than climbing. It is terribly easy to lose your balance, which each of us did a couple of times. Fortunately we fell just right and were not hurt. It was only mid afternoon when we reached camp but we decided we had enough for one day and saved the rest of the job for the next morning.

The tundra itself can make for difficult walking. It is mostly made up of grasses and a great variety of berry bushes: blueberries, cranberries, lingonberries, salmonberries, bunchberries and more; making for soft or spongy walking. On the other hand, much of the tundra is exposed gravel and has a hard surface, easy for walking. In most cases, the trails caribou, moose, bear and other animals have been using for thousands of years are easily visible and if the trail is leading in the direction you want to go, it makes for the best walking. Many of the small airplanes in Alaska are equipped with large tundra tires instead of pontoons. They not only work on most level tundra but they also work well on ocean beaches.

We have talked several times about leaving meat unattended, sometimes for days. It may surprise you to hear that in all our years of hunting big game in Alaska we have never lost any of our meat to predators and have had almost zero spoilage. However, one time we dressed out a caribou and left it over night to butcher because it was late in the day and we were so far from camp. When we returned in the morning we found several seagulls attacking the exposed hind quarters. We probably lost about ten pounds of meat.

Speaking of predators, we have encountered very few wolves and only shot one. Don Hester and Ed Morey were hunting together when Ed shot our largest caribou bull – ever. They packed all the meat back to camp but left the antlers for the next day. As they approached the carcass that next morning a black arctic wolf was working on the rib cage. The animal was so occupied with eating that he did not see the men approach. Ed was having some vision problems so he urged Don to shoot. Don did and dropped the wolf in its tracks. The pelt was "jet black" and made a gorgeous trophy. We have seen a few wolves while flying over the tundra, but never more than a "family size" pack. Several times we have seen wolves hiding and lying in wait for herds of caribou. Only once did we see them attack, and that was on a straggler that had dropped behind the herd.

And speaking of arctic wolves, the picture on the opposite page is of the largest wolf pelt, by far, I have ever seen. One of our bush pilots, Sonny Hedlund, shot it from his plane in the winter (legal at that time). Sonny's Eskimo mother was going to make me a seal skin parka and I had paid her a deposit of $300. She became ill, however, and was unable to do it. Sonny suggested that I could have the wolf pelt if his mother could keep the deposit. This particular pelt was nearly twice as large as the dozen or more he had hanging in his shed. Sonny said that the wolf weighed 205 pounds, and I believe him! (I am told it is no where near a record.)

In conclusion, one last caribou story. Seven of us had been out in camp the better part of a week and had not done very well. We each had filled a tag but four of the fellows had bought extra licenses and we had returned to the lodge at Iliamna with them not being filled. we had planned to fish a couple of days in the Newhalen River before heading home. There were only about 14 miles of roads at that time at Iliamna, mostly connecting the Eskimo village, the lodges, and the airport. We had driven in Paul's van to the waterfall — our favorite spot for rainbows, Dolly Vardens and grayling. We had two rifles with us in case of a problem with a bear. We had a good fishing trip and had just started back towards the lodge when a fairly large herd of caribou, about 30, started crossing the road in front of us. When they saw our vehicle they turned around and ran back out of sight. Thinking they might return, we hid the van behind the next hill and the four men with the unfilled extra licenses took the two rifles and positioned themselves out of sight. It wasn't long before the seven mature bulls in the herd showed up. Our hunters had no trouble dropping four nice animals. The rest of the herd, by the way, ran past the van! We were told back at the lodge that caribou rarely travel through this area.

The pelt of a 200 pound plus arctic wolf, 92 inches from the tip of the nose to the tip of the tail.

Kenny Zetah and Don Hester with Kenny's first caribou.

Denny Hanson and the antlers from the four Iliamna bulls that tried to cross the road to the Iliamna airport.

I know I just said, "One last story", but here's another short one I'd better share.

It doesn't happen very often in that wide open tundra country that a hunter hears caribou before he sees them, but that is exactly what happened on my most recent caribou hunt. We were camped on the shores of a nameless lake on the Alaskan Peninsula. On the first day of the hunt we saw a lot of animals but always in the distance. When we tried sneaking on them they seemed to sense our presence and managed to stay consistently out of range or just disappeared altogether. The morning of the second day I announced that I had walked too much that first day and planned to hunt close to camp and rest a bit. I confidently proclaimed, "I'm going to let them find me!"

Now, the caribou is the only animal I know that when it walks or runs makes a noise like bones "clunking" together. Depending on the number of animals, the noise can be heard more than 100 feet away. I have heard several explanations as to what makes the noise – everything from leg bones or ankle bones or knee joints to their cloven hoofs snapping together as they raise their feet off the ground.

After the other hunters were gone and I had cleaned up the breakfast dishes, I walked to a spot about 100 yards from camp where I had a good view of the lake shore and tundra area beyond. By sitting in a small brushy area I was pretty well hidden. Just before noon when I was thinking about walking back to camp and making a sandwich, I heard the peculiar but easily recognized noise the caribou bones make when they are on the move; and I knew there was more than one animal and I knew they were close behind me. I froze with rifle ready. They didn't smell me and if they saw me they apparently were not alarmed, because they suddenly, all seven of them, appeared about thirty yards to my right, moving at a slow trot. As I raised my rifle, they stopped and just looked at me. There were two respectable bulls; I chose the one with antlers with a double shovel. A single shot from my .300 mag. did the job.

IN SUMMARY
WHAT I HAVE LEARNED IN TWENTY FIVE YEARS OF HUNTING CARIBOU

When to Hunt

It has been our experience that the best time to hunt caribou in Alaska is from late August to mid September. Earlier than that, the animals still have velvet on their antlers and the weather may be too warm to keep the meat from spoiling. There will also be more insects, which, besides being a nuisance, may keep the animals at a high elevation. Later than that, the weather can be miserable. Even during the time slot I have identified, water often freezes in our pails overnight.

Where to Hunt

Caribou are found, generally, all over the state. The huge herds, in the thousands, are farther north and therefore less accessible. But apart from the spectacular experience of seeing so many animals, there is no real advantage in numbers when all you are looking for is one that is in killing range. Most caribou are probably shot in southwestern Alaska, the Alaska Range and the Brooks Range. We have done most of our hunting on the Alaska Peninsula and have flown out from lodges on Lake Iliamna and Lake Clark. Although caribou are hunted along roads and highways, we have always enjoyed fly-ins to remote areas where the only hunters you see are members of your own party. It is also true, that the more remote the area the less spooky the animals.

Is a Guide Necessary?

Currently, at this writing, guides for hunting caribou are not required in most areas, but for the first trip or two it is a good idea to have one. For trips after that, outfitters are available all over the state who can provide equipment like tents, cooking stoves, lanterns, packboards, food, etc., that you won't have to bring from home. They can also arrange air transportation. The outfitter or the pilot (and often they are the same individual) will know where the caribou are to be found.

What Do You Need to Bring from Home?

Bring at least two changes of clothing. Just assume it will rain at some point and it is very important to stay dry — so bring rain gear. An air mattress and sleeping bag (I like goose down) are critical but may be available from your guide or outfitter. For most locations, hip boots are a necessity, but also bring a comfortable pair of leather boots or "packs". Camo clothing is most common but it is a good idea to have at least one item of blaze orange in case there are other hunters in the area.

A good pair of binoculars is a must, the smaller and lighter the better. Bring a compass but establishing landmarks as you walk is equally important. A GPS can be very valuable.

There is a good chance you will be camped on a lake or stream that has fish, so bring along a rod, reel and appropriate tackle for trout and northern pike. This will give you something to do if you get your caribou early in the hunt and the change in menu will be appreciated by your partners.

Which Rifle?

Whatever you use for deer will work for caribou. I suppose the 30-06 is most common. If you are like me, you will want something bigger in case bear are a problem. That is why I carry a .300 mag. I feel a bolt action is the more dependable in an emergency but many argue that an automatic is better because it is faster and doesn't require as much dexterity or thinking. The truth is, we have never been threatened by a bear except one time we thought we were being stalked but nothing happened. It has been our habit to sleep with one, and only one, loaded rifle in the tent.

Is a Bow a Practical Alternative?

You bet! Neither I nor any of my caribou hunting partners use a bow, but on most trips I have been within good arrow range of a caribou, and that's without trying to get closer.

What Will I Need to Butcher My Animal and Protect My Meat?

As I mentioned in my stories, all you really need to butcher an animal is a stout, sharp knife, but if you haven't had that experience, bring along a collapsible meat saw. Also, bring along cloth meat bags to keep off any flies. Blow Flies will lay eggs in raw meat and maggots will soon hatch.

We leave the hide on for protection. Sheets of plastic often come in handy when camping, like on the floor of your tent, but it can also be used to cover meat when it rains.

Any Tips on the Actual Hunting?

The foregoing stories were chosen to do just that, to tell you what you need to know, but there are a few points worth reviewing:

- Caribou are not as shy as white tail deer and their vision isn't as keen, but they do have an excellent nose. Watch the wind! Keep it in your face.

- Watch constantly; caribou seem to appear right out of the ground.

- If you watch the wind and take advantage of any cover, you can sneak on caribou.

- If caribou are on the move, you probably can't catch-up. Your better chance may be to guess where they are headed and try to cut them off.

- If you get tired of walking, choose a place to sit where you have a good view and where you, yourself, are not highly visible.

- Use your binoculars – a lot!

- Although there usually are a lot of berries, bring a light lunch with you (at least candy bars) and something to drink. Pond water can be contaminated. Streams and rivers are safer but there are no guarantees – especially in beaver country.

- Most of the time we hunt in pairs. It's just a lot more fun to be with someone on a long day of hunting.

Safety First!
Bring a first aid kit and appropriate medications.

In over twenty-five Alaskan hunts we have never had anyone become ill or seriously injured, but it does happen. Be sure that your pilot or outfitter checks on you every two or three days. Sometimes a fly-over is all that is needed but agree on some kind of a signal in advance that the pilot can easily see if you want him to land. Cell phones work in some areas, your outfitter or guide will know which.

Stay Legal

Licenses are required. Also, as in other states, regulations will vary. Your guide or outfitter should be aware of any restrictions. Remember, you are required to salvage all of the meat on a big game animal, including the rib meat. Also, the antlers must be brought out last.

Chapter 2
MOOSE HUNTING

Jack Nelsen, who shot the moose, and his proud father, Dean.

The rack from my first Alaska moose, as displayed in my cabin on the Lake of the Woods in Ontario.

Moose found anywhere in the world are big animals, but moose found in Alaska are enormous. Likewise, their antlers are huge.

On my first few caribou hunts in Alaska, we had not seen moose, although we were told they were nearby in the woods and brushy areas along the rivers and streams. On most of our later hunts, we have been in areas of the Alaska Peninsula where both moose and caribou are common. The fact that our guide and outfitter, Paul Carlson, had transported an ATV and trailer to the area we hunted encouraged us to try for moose along with the caribou. Because of their size, packing moose meat to places where a float plane can pick them up is just an awful lot of work. With an ATV available, that would not be a problem. It is true that a lot of Alaskan moose are packed out, but that is not a job for older hunters.

I shall never forget my first Alaskan moose. On the very first day of the hunt, Paul had suggested that I position myself on a high bank overlooking the Lower Talarec Creek (which is really a small river). There was an abundance of willows and alders on both sides of the creek and even a few trees, but I would be able to see any animals within a mile of where I was sitting.

I don't think I had been there more than a few minutes when I glanced to my right and saw a bull moosee standing on the top of the same high bank I was sitting on, facing me. I had hunted moose in Canada, several times, but I recall my feeling of disbelief at the animal's size. His legs, in particular, seemed so long. And it was only about a hundred yards away. I took aim at its huge chest where I thought it would do the most damage to its lungs and hopefully its heart, and fired. What happened next has been imprinted on my mind forever. I can see it even now as I sit here at my computer! The moose collapsed, but instead of staying on top of the hill, it rolled, head over heels, all the way down the steep bank. There was mud and soft earth at the bottom of the hill and one of its huge antlers was fully imbedded in the ground! Try to imagine such a huge animal falling well over 100 feet down the steep hillside.

Two of my hunting partners that trip, Urban Abendroth and Don Hester, heard me shoot and soon arrived on the scene. With their help we butchered the trophy. We agreed that the ATV couldn't possibly navigate the high hill and that we'd have to bring it to the top on a packboard. It was my animal, so I knew the packboard would be on my back. The hill was so steep I could not stand up and walk up the hill, so I crawled on my hands and knees with one of my partners in front pulling on my coat collar and the other crawling behind and pushing, sometimes on the bottom of the load and other times on my rear end. We made eight trips that way!

Paul had heard my shot back in camp and arrived with the ATV/trailer combination shortly before we brought the last load up the hill. As Don put it, "Paul was a sight for sore eyes." The moose's rack (on the opposite page) is displayed in my cabin on the Lake of the Woods.

In the chapter on caribou hunting I talked about lessons learned when Bob Mayhew had not checked his scope after arriving in camp and the result was hitting the wrong animal. Apparently I had forgotten the lesson on a moose trip several years later, as you will see.

Urban and I had teamed up on this particular day, I walked the bottom land along a stream and he walked the ridge a hundred feet or so higher. After about an hour of this walking I happened to glance up at Urban and saw that he was standing still, had dropped his rifle and was facing me with his arms above his head, made to look like antlers!

I knew he was trying to tell me that there was a moose in between us. I could see nothing, so I advanced slowly in his direction. Suddenly, a respectable animal walked through the brush and trees, coming directly towards me. I think we saw each other about the same time, because we both stopped, about 125 yards apart. Without hesitation, I took aim at its huge chest with my .300 mag. and pulled the trigger. To my dismay, it wheeled around and disappeared into the cover from which it came before I could throw another shell into the chamber. I broke through the brush in a couple of minutes and was relieved to see the moose just standing there in a fairly large, but shallow, puddle of water. Just then, Urban's rifle cracked and the animal went down, this time very much dead.

As I approached our trophy I couldn't wait to see where I had hit it and figure out why it hadn't gone down immediately. As I searched in vain for a bullet hole, Urban walked up and said, "I think you'll find you broke its left hind leg."

Sure enough. the leg was broken at the knee. But I couldn't find anywhere that the bullet could have passed through the body.

Urban added, "It was having trouble walking; it was dragging that leg. It never did run. It was just standing still when I finished it off."

It was then that it dawned on me that my scope could have been off. Sure enough, when I tried it out it missed the target completely. I had to resort to a huge target because it was off about three feet at 125 yards! I was just lucky that I hit the moose at all!

The next year I began transporting my rifle in a hard-cover case, even in the pontoon plane.

We learned another lesson on this trip; moose, because of their huge size and weight are not like other big game that may still travel at full speed after being hit hard. I remember one Minnesota white tail deer that had three legs broken and was still moving when we caught up to it.

Although I learned my lesson to check my scope after transporting my rifle in any vehicle, even as good and careful a guide as Paul Carlson had a similar problem. In fact, it was the very next year.

Paul always wanted us to shoot our own animals, but we had come to the last full day of the hunt and were still short a couple of moose. We wanted at least one more animal, so we prevailed on Paul to help out. I had taken a stand along a fairly wide but shallow stream where I had a good view of the moose pasture and where we had shot moose in previous years. Paul crossed the stream and used a huge rock for cover, about a mile from me, but in very good view. Another member of our party, who shall go nameless because he could seldom sit still for more than an hour, had agreed to take a position a couple of miles up-steam and stay put as long as he could, and then drive the brush and scrub trees that grew along the river, in our direction,

I was surprised that mid-morning came and we hadn't seen our driver, but about that time a very nice bull came out of the cover, walking directly towards the rock which Paul was using for a hiding place. It turned out that our driver had spooked the animal. As the bull got withing range it veered off at right angles to Paul, but giving him a nice broadside shot. I saw the bull "hump" before I heard Paul's shot, but the moose didn't go down. It just stood there. Paul fired again and again, but there was no sign he had hit the animal. Paul then started to walk in the bull's direction, firing occasionally as he drew nearer. The bull still just stood there, Finally, Paul walked up almost to the bull, in point blank range, and fired what we learned later was his ninth and last bullet he had taken with him when he left camp that morning! The bull moose dropped in its tracks – dead.

About that time, the driver appeared into view and I crossed the river (we were all wearing hip boots). We arrived at Paul and his fallen trophy about the same time. Needless to say, we gave our guide a very bad time, but he was completely mystified. He just kept saying, "How could I hit him my first shot and then miss the next seven?"

I suggested that it had to be his scope. He had a fixed scope on his Weatherby and couldn't tip it off and use open sights. Later, when Paul acquired more ammunition back at camp, he found I had guessed right, it was his scope. "But then," I asked, "how could you have hit him and hit him in a vital spot, with your first shot?"

Paul, a deeply religious man, answered sincerely, "The good Lord must have made me lead the bull way too far."

I'm sure Paul was more protective of his scope after that, but he never did resort to a hard case for his rifle.

The very next year, I was sitting at the very same spot on the river where I had witnessed Paul's difficulty in killing his moose, but perhaps a little later in the day. I was surprised to see Lloyd Olson appear down stream on my side of the river. I whistled to get his attention, but the noise of the water apparently made it impossible for him to hear me. It really wasn't all that important that we connect so I just watched him cross the river and then headed for "Paul's rock".

The rack of the bull moose I shot on the sandbar now graces the space above my garage door where I live on the Crow Wing River in Minnesota

Lloyd was less than half way there when a beautiful bull stepped into the water at the exact same place where Lloyd had crossed. Over the years I have seen several deer follow my tracks or those of another hunter, but never a moose. Lloyd said later that he had been following a game trail for easier walking and that was probably what the moose was doing when the hunted appeared to be following the hunter.

Anyway, the moose was in nice range for me, a little over 100 yards. There was a sandbar about a third of the way across the steam and when the bull reached the dry ground I fired. I can still see the huge animal slowly collapse! I didn't need a second shot. Once down the bull never stirred.

Lloyd, of course heard the shot, but only after the animal was down. It was only after he saw me get up and start towards the sandbar that he realized there was an animal down. As he walked up within conversation distance, he observed, "I guess when we tell hunters they need to look in all directions that also means behind you!"

With Lloyd's help the butchering didn't take long, but the ATV arrived before we were through and because the stream was shallow, Paul wa able to drive right up to the animal. On some other Alaskan hunts and when hunting in Canada, we would loved to have had that convenience. I should say though, that when hunting in the Cumberland House, Saskatchewan, area we were blessed with guides who were descendants of the French voyagers and they were built for packing meat and never complained or worried about how far we were from camp or the boat. Most of them could even trot with a quarter of moose on their shoulders.

Talking about moose hunting on a river reminds me of the first year Francis Zetah and his then teenage son, Kenny, hunted with us. It was the first day of the hunt and at my suggestion the father and son walked to a river bottom about a mile from camp to post for moose or caribou that might come along. About mid morning I decided to check on them. Because of the wide open tundra country they weren't hard to spot. When I was close enough for conversation I asked, "See anything?"

They both started talking at once about a bull moose that had walked by just across the river.

"Well, I didn't hear you shoot," I responded.

"Well, no," Francis then explained, "I wouldn't let Kenny shoot because I didn't think we could get across the river to get the meat."

"I guess I should have told you," I said in embarrassment, "the river may be wide but I don't think it's more than knee deep anywhere around here!"

A lot of moaning and groaning followed.

I learned that the moose had disappeared into pretty large grove of trees and brush that grew all along the far side of the river. I naturally felt quite badly that when I suggested they sit by the river I hadn't explained that animals could be shot on either side of the stream and retrieved relatively easily. So I volunteered to cross the stream and make a big circle around the area where the moose was heading in the hope of spooking it back in range of the Zetahs.

As I waded across I stopped several times to make sure the others could see that in most places the water was more like ankle deep rather than knee deep. Once on the other shore I made my circle through the cover, hoping that the moose had stopped to eat or rest before going too far. I suppose I had walked, slowly, for about an hour when I stopped to survey a high hill back on the Zetah's side of the river that started its rise nearly a mile up stream and quite a ways back from the river. At that moment, a bull moose appeared, trotting up that hill, which was really a small mountain but not quite high enough for snow. The hill was covered with tundra, no trees or brush, so the moose was very visible. I just hoped the other hunters saw it.

Just at the moose was disappearing over the crest of the hill, I could see Kenny running up the hill. He was clearly running faster than the moose was moving but I was afraid he would "run out of gas" before he caught up with the animal. However, teenagers have a lot of stamina and spurred on by an adrenaline rush he never slowed down while in my sight. Shortly after he went over the top I heard a barrage of rifle shots.

Now there's an old hunters' saying back in Minnesota, "One shot, one deer; many shots, no deer!" But this wasn't Minnesota and Kenny got his moose.

In the story we just finished, the son got the moose, but I am reminded of another father-son combination where the son emptied his rifle at a bull but he was lucky to have his father near by to finish it off. Urban Abendroth and his teenage son were hunting several hundred yards apart. When Urban heard the barrage of rifle fire he wasn't in a position where he could see his son, so he hurried in that direction and to a spot where he would have a better view. He told us later that he was just in time to see the bull running at full speed for a heavy thicket of mature alders. Urban just had time for one shot as the bull entered the brush. He went on to say, "It looked like when I hit him he took a big jump right into the thicket."

Having heard all the shooting I made my way to "the battlefield". I'm glad I did, or I would have had a hard time believing what I saw. The bull, and it was a big one, was dead but suspended in the thicket with all four feet off the ground! We literally had to chop and saw the trees and bushes down so we could butcher the animal.

The boy had hit the bull pretty well but I would guess father and son are still arguing as to whether the father's help was necessary or if dad had hit the bull at all!

There are other great memories of Alaska moose hunts, like the time Chet Snyder had a running, long shot at a nice bull that was headed for a big beaver pond. He hit the animal several times but not in a vital enough place. Finally, after it had run about a hundred yards into the knee deep water (the moose's knees, not ours), the bull went down, dead. I was the only hunter near Chet and therefore the only one who showed up to help with the butchering. Unfortunately, I was wearing leather boots. Chet was so kind as to insist I put on his hip boots and he slipped into my leathers.

There was no way we could pull the moose to dry ground and we knew the water was too deep for the ATV, which wasn't available until much later anyway. Chet and I are both pretty big guys and we were able to wrestle one quarter of the moose at a time, using the moose's long legs for leverage, onto a dry hump along side the animal. And then we were able to drag one butchered quarter at a time onto dry ground on the edge of the pond.

Chet never would admit that his feet were cold; he insisted that all the hard work kept even his feet warm.

It was on that same trip that Chet and I had an amusing experience back at the Eskimo village (Iliamna) after the hunt. We came across a very old native lady sitting on a bench in the village. She was so wrinkled she looked a hundred years old and was so picturesque in her traditional dress and head scarf. Chet asked if he could sit by her and have their picture taken.

She said nothing. But Chet handed me his camera anyway and sat down, boldly putting his arm around her. I snapped the picture and Chet got up, simply saying, "Thank you, very much."

The Eskimo lady then put her hand out and said, "Twenty dollars."

Chet and I both laughed as he started to pull out his billfold. But then she added, "Just kidding!"

Chet responded, "You really fooled us. It was worth twenty dollars," and laid a bill of that denomination on the bench!

There was another moose hunting experience that was a bit unique. Don Hester and Paul Carlson had set up camp the day before the rest of us flew in. That evening, Don walked a couple of hundred yards from camp to a small hill with a good view. The area beyond was mostly open tundra, but there were nearby areas of brush and trees that looked like good moose cover. Don was ready for either caribou or moose.

Shortly before dark, a bull moose emerged from a brushy area and appeared headed for a grove of cottonwoods. It was a long shot, but Don connected. There was just enough daylight to butcher the animal and transport it back to camp with the ATV.

The next day, three of us flew into the small lake on which Don and Paul had made camp. Don suggested to one of the newcomers, Ted Lelwica, that he might want to post just over the hill where he (Don) had shot the moose the night before, (in those days you could hunt the same day you flew). Don added, "You should be able to see the rib cage and other remains of my moose."

That sounded like a good idea to Ted, so he picked up his rifle and climbed the hill in back of camp. After sitting quite awhile without any action, Ted decided to take a look at the remains of Don's moose, except he couldn't see them – anywhere. But he did see a peculiar looking pile of gravel. As he approached it he realized that a bear had apparently covered the remains of the moose with gravel and loose tundra! It was then that he also saw the bear, a big old grizzly, not too far away.

When Ted returned to camp later and told us his story, we all had the same questions on our minds, "When would the bear return to finish his meal?" And, secondly, "Should we move camp?"

After considerable discussion we decided to stay where we were but keep our eyes open. Five days later when we broke camp, the bear had still not returned.

CALLING MOOSE

You may have noticed, that I have made no mention of calling moose. That is because none of us, including our guide, Paul Carlson, felt competent in that skill. I, for one, have had moose answer my amateurish calls, but they have never come to me. On the other hand, I have been on several guided hunts in Canada where the guides were proficient in calling moose and it has been very productive. And it is a special experience to have a moose respond and to hear it draw near.

There are many guides who can call moose in Alaska and there is no doubt that is a very effective way of hunting them.

One such person is my friend, Dean Nelsen, from my home town of Staples, Minnesota. Dean has been an Alaskan citizen for several years and earns his living as a pilot and guide. His family is still in Staples and he returns regularly to see them. Actually, as I write this book, Dean has all three of his children in Alaska on an extended fishing trip. When his son, Jack, was ten years old, he joined his father for his first ever moose hunt. The picture at the start of this chapter is of father and son and Jack's record trophy. But let's let Jack tell the story in his own words!

Jack Nelsen from Staples, Minnesota, with the second biggest rack every shot in Alaska.

CALLING MOOSE
BY JACK NELSEN

Hello! My name is Jack Frances Nelsen. I live in Staples, MN with my mom, Valerie; brother, Ben and my sister Autumn. I am ten years old and go to fifth grade at Staples Elementary School. My dad, Dean Nelsen, lives and works in Fairbanks, Alaska. We used to live in Alaska also until about four years ago.

Moose hunting is something I had dreamed of since dad brought home the first big moose from one of his hunts. I was too young to moose hunt at the time, but dad did take me Caribou hunting with a snowmobile. I was too small to shoot but I did have fun riding along. So you can imagine my excitement when dad invited me to hunt with him for moose with three of his other friends.

My trip started September 16, 2004 when Rod and Lee, two of my dad's friends I would be hunting with, picked me up from school in Staples. We had to drive to the twin-cities (Minneapolis/St. Paul, MN) for the airplane ride to Alaska. On the drive, my job was to finish my homework. We also stopped at two stores to pick up last minute stuff for the hunt; chips and Gatorade. I liked that. After we parked at the airport we had to get a shuttle-bus to finish the drive to the airport. Finally we made it. I really had to go to the bathroom. Then the long wait for the right airplane began. Fortunately, it only took 30 minutes before we were able to get on the Northwest flight. When we found our seats and the Captain said that the flight would take 5 hours and 11 minutes to get to Anchorage, AK. About halfway through the flight we got pop and our choice of chicken or lasagna; I picked lasagna. We finally made it to Alaska.

I was surprised when we got off of the airplane, there was my dad waiting for us. We went to his office and checked our bags with his airline; Frontier Flying Service. Dad works as a pilot for them. And they were going to fly us out to Aniak, AK the next morning. Then we went out for dinner at Chili's with my dad and his friends; Lee and Ron who would be hunting with us and several more of his work-friends. It was awesome, I got a chicken sandwich. After that we went to a very nice hotel to sleep. Most people don't go there because it is very expensive.

The next morning we went to my dad's office at the Anchorage air-port about 7:00 a.m. We got our stuff and boarded the Beech 1900 air-plane to fly to Aniak, AK. Aniak is where we used to live when I was in Alaska. It was only a one-hour flight. When we got to Aniak we organized our gear and took one more flight, which was only 30 min-utes long to a smaller runway. Then we got on a smaller single prop airplane to fly out to the middle of no-where Alaska. It took two air-plane trips for all of our stuff to make it. Dad went on the first trip with Ron, as only he knew where we could land and he needed to show the pilot. I went on the second trip with Rod and Lee and the rest of the gear.

It was time to set up camp. We set up camp right next to a river. After I finished helping everyone I couldn't resist and had to go fishing. I caught an Artic Grayling on my very first cast. Then I caught ten grayling on my first ten casts, it was fun. I caught a lot of grayling the first night but no other types of fish. Then it was time to get ready for bed. Right before bed we went to survey the moose territory. We walked down the gravel bar we were camped on. Dad was calling for moose to see if he could get a response before we went to bed. No luck.

The next morning it was time to go hunting. Rod and Lee went up river, Rod went up a little creek that ran into our river and Dad and I walked down river. We left around 9:00 a.m. and walked about a mile down river. Dad was calling for moose as we walked, but we didn't hear anything. There were lots of grizzly bear and wolf tracks along the banks of the river. Down river we climbed up a cliff to sit and moose call. After about thirty minutes it was time to walk back to camp and see if anybody else saw a moose. At the bottom of the cliff Dad called one last time. This time, he got a response. I didn't hear the bull as I was skipping rocks into the river. But Dad called again, I heard the bull grunt back this time. We ran back up to the top of the cliff just in time to see the bull come over the mountain across the river. It was Huge. The bull looked our direction from the mountain. I was very excited. The bull then went down into the trees but kept calling. After 10 minutes it got very quite and we thought we lost him. But no, he started to grunt again. This time he was ripping up trees and busting up stuff like crazy. At this point I was very, very, very excited. The bull got quiet again and gave one little soft grunt, my dad called back softly. I don't know what dad said in moose talk, but here came the bull. The bull walked right toward us pushing over trees and tearing up brush on the way. I was bouncing up and down I was so excited. Dad kept telling me to take it easy. The bull stopped on the other side of the river about 80 to 100 yards away looking right at us.

We couldn't find anything to rest the gun on so I could shoot so Dad held my beaver chewed walking stick in his right hand, up-right like a tree. I put the gun on his arm then and put the moose in the scope. It was really, really big now. Dad said he didn't want the moose to cross the river and we would have to shoot if it started to cross. The moose took a drink of water, looked up at us and started to cross the river. Dad said put the cross-hairs between his ears and when it looked good; SHOOT! I put the cross hairs on his head right in the middle and boom. When the smoke cleared he was dead, not to move again, only a twitch of his legs still remained. I don't remember this next part but Dad say's I gave him the gun and ran along the top of the cliff jumping up and down and screaming something about a big moose. But the moose was on the other side of the river so we could not go see him right away. We had to walk back to camp to change into our waders and float back down with the raft.

It took about two hours to finally make it back to the moose to find out how big it was. Dad and Rod but the tape to it, it measured 76 3/4 inches. Nobody believed the tape. So they measured the bull again. My Dad was just walking circles around the moose saying "Oh my Gawd".

Then we started to skin it. I helped as much as I could but it was big. So with Dad and Rod cleaning the moose I went fishing for artic grayling, it was quite fun. After the moose was cleaned we built a platform out of small trees to help support the moose in the raft. Then the hard part. We had to push the raft with the whole moose back up river to our camp. It took us about an hour to push the moose one mile up river. We almost didn't make it as the river had one fast spot. I pulled a rope on one side of the river tied to the raft. Rod pulled a rope on the other side of the river tie to the raft and Dad pushed the raft from behind. I was really tired.

The next day Dad called a friend on a satellite phone to come pick my moose up with his Husky airplane. It took him two trips to get all of the moose out of camp.

The rest of the hunt we floated down the river. I went fishing every day. And on the last day of the hunt my Dad called in a bull moose for Rod that measured 67 1/2 inches. The moose came out of the

Note the bullet hole in the center of the forehead!

brush on the gravel bar twenty feet away. Rod wasn't going to shoot, and then he did. The bull ran a little ways, but Rod shot again paralyzing then killing it. It was a perfect spot to set up camp for the night and wait for the boat to pick us up the next morning for the ride down river to the airport.

My moose has been officially scored at 255 1/2 inches B & C making it number two (2) all time in the world. Nobody can believe it. I really want to go moose hunting again but my Dad say's it my brother Ben's turn next.

For more information check out Jack's website at
www.jacksantlers.com

HUNTING BY DRIFTING STREAMS

Drifting streams or rivers can be one of the more productive ways of hunting moose in Alaska. Not all streams go through moose country, but guides and outfitters are "paid to know." They can also tell you if the stream is deep enough to use a small outboard. In some streams, outboard jet motors work best.

We have never used this technique of moose hunting but several of my friends have, and have done very well. Providing you "shoot to kill", you can avoid packing the meat long distances.

But then again, you can get fooled. Jerel Nelsen, of my community (Staples, MN) was on his first moose hunt with his brother Dean (the Alaskan pilot and guide mentioned in the previous episode) and they chose to hunt on the Anvik River in west-central Alaska. As they rounded a bend in the river, there stood a cow and a nice legal bull in the water, near mid-stream. On one side of the river was a sandbar, an ideal place to butcher an animal. On the opposite side was a high bank. Dean opted to follow the high bank side in the hope of spooking the bull onto the sandbar. As if the bull sensed the strategy it opted for the high bank. By the time the hunters were so close all Jerel could see through his 3-power scope was hair! But after adjusting the scope he had a perfect shot at the left shoulder as the bull was leaving the river. Dean and Jerel agreed that he had made a killing shot, but they thought it best to let the animal lie down and die or at least stiffen up. So they pulled into shore and had a leisurely lunch. They were surprised, however, when they took up the trail after lunch, how far the moose had gone before it came into view, lying down. As it got up, Jerel shot it in the right shoulder, but the moose just turned and started to run away, so this time, Jerel shot it in the back of the head. The bull reared up and then fell over backwards – dead.

But imagine their surprise and disappointment when they discovered the moose had fallen into fairly deep water on the far side of an oxbow, which had at one time been the river bed. The water was so deep they had to walk around it – and then began the horrendous job of wrestling the moose into position for butchering. Had it not been for the water hazard, it would still have been a fairly long haul back to the boat, but the oxbow meant that they had to walk around it to get back to the river – well over a mile!

The rack measured 65 inches, a nice trophy and a lot of good eating, but at the moment they weren't sure it was all worthwhile. So much for the river hunting being easy.

Now the fun begins!

Jerel Nelsen with his trophy back in camp. Maybe it was worthwhile after all!

Moose are usually not dangerous animals to hunt, but cows with calves and bulls in the rut have been known to be problems. Several years ago, when it was still legal to fly and shoot the same day, a dentist who made regular visits to the village of Iliamna, hired a pilot to help him get a trophy bull. They spotted a nice animal and the pilot dropped the dentist off to stalk him, saying that he would return in a few hours to help pack the meat.Shortly after the plane took off the dentist was surprised to encounter a much smaller bull with a harem of cows; the trophy bull was nowhere in site. The bull promptly made a couple of false charges. The dentist didn't want to shoot the smaller animal but ended up climbing a handy tree! The bull eventually left with his harem, but when the dentist thought it was safe to climb down, the bull returned. They kept up this game until it was nearly time for the pilot to return. The dentist did want some moose meat for the winter, so he finally shot the smaller bull!

Chapter 3
SHEEP HUNTING

Jack Nelsen and his Dall Sheep

I have personally not hunted sheep, but here is a story of Don Hester's and Paul Carlson's successful hunt.

The rest of us had to return to Minnesota, but Don, being already retired at that time, wanted to stay on and try for a Dall sheep. Paul had not guided many sheep hunters but he knew there was a pretty good herd up on one of the mountains bordering Lake Clark, In fact, it was possible to see them occasionally through binoculars from out on the lake.

They packed provisions for a four day hunt, including a tent, of course, and had a pilot drop off everything from the air at the source of a dry creek that wandered down the mountain to the shore of the lake. Then the pilot dropped the hunters off on the shore where the creek entered the lake. All the men had to carry was their rifles. It was still a difficult climb, but the men took their time and made it to where their provisions had been dropped off by the plane in a little over two hours.

Don and Paul sat down for a well-deserved rest, but they said that only minutes after they sat down they saw something white moving through the brush only about 50 or 60 yards away. Their rifles were already loaded so they just sat there, very still, and waited. Several sheep suddenly walked into the clear (the men never could agree as to how many, seven or eight). They had agreed at the start of the trip that if they saw any sheep, Don should take the first shot. So when a ram with a full curl stepped out, Don let him have it. As Don said later, "At that close range it was a piece of cake."

The sheep collapsed on the first shot and never moved. Paul chose the next biggest, a nice sheep with a three-quarter curl. By now, of course, the animals were in a full flight back into the brush, but Paul got off a couple of shots. The sheep ran about 40 yards but the men had no trouble finding it.

After butchering and carefully "capeing out" their trophies, they decided they could easily make it back down to the lake before dark. Using their cell phone they were able to relay a message to the pilot to pick them up. They decided to leave their provisions and equipment there and hire a couple of younger guys to retrieve them. As it turned out, when word spread of their successful hunt, a couple of locals volunteered for the job in the hope of also getting sheep. Ironically, even after four days they didn't see any sign of sheep!

Jack Nelsen and his Dall Sheep

The sheep were heavy animals and the trip down proved more difficult than the climb up, but the men took their time with frequent rest stops, and made it down to the lake in just under four hours.

But you can bet they slept very well that night!

Both sheep were mounted – they are gorgeous!

Just two years after Jack Nelsen shot the huge moose in the previous story, he shot the beautiful Dall sheep pictured on the title page of this chapter and above. But let's let Jack tell his own story. Jack's now twelve years old.

SHEEP HUNT
BY JACK NELSEN

It all started on a foggy mid-August day in Dead Horse, Alaska, with my dad, our friends Lona and Bill and me. Lona had worked in Dead Horse so she knew many people there. We could not fly out to sheep camp for three days because of bad weather.

Finally we had good enough weather, with 600 foot ceiling and 5 miles of flight visibility, so we were able to fly out of Dead Horse to a small airstrip called Kavik about 80 miles south and east of Dead Horse. Dan Sailors, a friend of my dads, met us in Kavik and flew us out in a Husky airplane, which is like a super cub, to the Canning River another 50 miles south and east of Kavik in the Brooks Range where we started our hunt. That night, after setting up base camp, dad, Lona and I started our hike up the valley where we hoped to set up a spike camp and find sheep. Bill stayed at the camp and watched for bears.

The first night we put up a spike camp about 2 miles from base camp. The next morning we got up early and had breakfast. We started hiking up the valley making about three miles when we saw five rams, one of which we thought was legal. We stayed there for the day so we would not scare them. We managed to make it up the creek bed about ten yards that night to a very small gravel bar. We set up camp there that night.

The next morning we did not see the sheep so we went up the creek bed to the creek drainage about three miles away that the sheep had gone up the day before. We snuck over the ridge and saw two sheep. Both were maybe legal so we went back down and on the back side of the ridge to try to get a better look at them. When we got up to the ridge we saw two other rams. Now we are thinking this is good. Just the sheep we were looking for.

We watched the rams for about an hour trying to get a better look at them. The first two we saw we were still considering, but the second two were much bigger. One of them was for sure a nice ram with a full curl and a quarter turn in his horns. We were getting serious about that one. We started to stalk him to a degree.

Then we went around a corner and saw seven rams. A couple of them were also legal. We still wanted the second two that we saw earlier so we went back down to the ridge where we first saw the two rams and started to wait.

We waited for about forty-five minutes to an hour before, to our surprise, the two rams started walking straight to us on the other side of the drainage. They stopped about four hundred yards away and again started toward us. I was shooting dad's 300 Browning Ultra Mag with 150 grain bullets. The bullets only drop about 4 inches at 400 yards making a long shot like that pretty easy.

Dad told me to just be comfortable before I shot. Lona was about five feet below me watching her ram. I said, "Can I shoot Dad?" I was comfortable. I saw my chance and before Dad could respond — Boom! I shot and it was a hit. Dad told me to reload, so I did and shot again. This time I hit him in the horn and put him to the ground.

Lona hit her ram right behind the shoulder which was a perfect shot. We had two beautiful Dall sheep rams dead.

We went down the ridge to our spike camp and got what we needed and then went to see our sheep. Lona's was a full curl and a bit taping out at 36 1/2 inches. then we went to mine. What a ram! A curl and a quarter! It was forty inches even on one side and 39 5/8 on the other side. Then we went back to Lona's and pulled hers back down to mine for pictures and butchering. We then started to skin them. While we were working, we saw a 7/8 curl ram bed down across the canyon watching us.

After that we went back to spike camp and put down the meat, hide and horns. We wanted to try to get one of the other rams my dad had seen to fill his tag. So we started the hike up the hill looking at every corner so we would not scare them. After a while we had a chance at the ram my dad was going after, but it just did not work. We went after them again, but the shot would have been about four hundred yards and he was on a shale ridge. The fall of the sheep would be bad so we decided to just say it was not worth it. We went back to spike camp to spend the night.

The next morning we opened the tent door to six inches of new snow on the ground. After finding clothes, boots and packs buried under the snow, we brought all the meat, hide and horns halfway back to base camp which was about eight miles away. We then went back to spike camp and spent the night again.

The next morning we brought spike camp all the way back to base camp. What a relief. We made hot meals and went to bed. The next morning Dad and Lona went back for the meat, hide and horns. Bill and I made a meat rack and did stuff around camp for the day until Dad and Lona made it back.

Boy, were they tired! They made hot meals which was Mountain House freeze dried food. The next day we sat in camp all day, fleshed and salted the sheep hides.

The next day we had a really nice bull caribou run right by camp as we waited for Dan Sailors to take us out. He had taken Lona to Happy Valley air strip the day before. Dan made it to base camp in time to fly us out to Kavik to catch an airplane to Dead Horse that night.

The next day we flew into Fairbanks on a Frontier Airline Beech 1900. The type of plane my dad flies. Sue, Bill's wife, had dinner ready. We had a great dinner.

The next day I left Fairbanks to go back to Minnesota to my mom, brother and sister.

THE END

Chapter 4
BEAR HUNTING

Rod Hafften and Lee Zalher with Rod's blonde brown bear. The bear was shot near the ocean's shore and the bear's huge head is resting on a commercial fishing buoy. The hunters are from Motley, MN.

PATIENCE AND PERSISTENCE
BY DEAN NELSEN

This is a true story not so much about hunting as the willingness to dream and the patience and persistence to make a dream come true. But I guess that is what hunting is.

Day seven of our fifth Alaskan Brown bear hunt began as the other six days had with Rod Hafften, his lady Lee Zalher and me, the guide, sitting on a sand dune 50 yards from the beach of the Bering Sea between the sea and the mouth of the Cathedral River located on the northern side of the Alaskan Peninsula. The Blonde Brownie rounded the bottom edge of far bluff about 1/2 mile up the beach as the 4:30 am sunrise dawned gray and muted with a low overcast washing out any color as the sun tried to turn night into day.

Five years of brown bear hunting memories entailing the three of us filtered through my mind as the bear made its way along the opposite bank of the river slowly but surely toward us. What to do? I thought of our first bear hunt sitting in a tent through a three day blizzard with Rod while the bears slept soundly under six feet of snow in the mountains surrounding us. The blizzard left us no opportunity to take a bear the first year.

We had seen a bear similar in size and color to the one just rounding the bluff on the first morning of our trip and had passed on it thinking it may be a female of only 7 1/2 to 8 feet in size. I thought of year two as Lee, Rod and I snow shoed 12 miles through rotten snow only to turn down a shot at a big brownie as there was no way we could retrieve and transport the bear back to camp if shot, a tough decision to make, but the correct one at the time. But now was day seven of year five with only two days of hunting left. What to do? Do we pass on this bear and potentially go home again empty handed?

Was it the same bear? It sure looked bigger under the gray light. But the blonde color phase is rare among brown bear and generally pre-disposed toward the females and this one was really blonde along the entire body except for dark chocolate on each leg giving the impression of a bear wearing stockings. We didn't want to take a female if we had a choice. I thought of year three with Rod and Lee when we didn't even make it into the bear country we wanted to hunt due to the spring snow conditions and bad weather. We ended up spending half of the hunt waiting out the weather in an aircraft hanger the other half hunting in low hills spotting only sows and cubs. Again no bears only dreams and desire to try again.

Boy, this bear sure does look good. Is it just the bad light or is it a good bear. The bear is moving closer now along the river. Decisions have to be made. What to do? I think of the bear we lost hunting during year four. It was a good bear. Rod had felt comfortable with the broad side shot as the three of us sat in the rain watching the bear feed along a river in Western Alaska. We searched for two days just knowing the shot was good and the bear was dead some where close, but if the shot was a fatal we never found the bear or any sign on it. I looked at Rod, he looked at me. The blonde brownie was at a point along the beach where a decision had to be made or the oppor-tunity would be lost. What to do?

Rod looked to Lee, our trip photographer and backbone for Rod through the past four years of Alaskan bear hunts and no bears. The decision was made to go for it; this bear was the one we had been waiting for all these years. With the memory of the lost bear in my mind the decision was made to shoot. The bear was in the open now working his way along the cut bank on the opposite side of the river.

The river bank was free of brush making follow up shots possible if needed. Rod placed the perfect shot at 100 yards. The bear was dead before any of us had a chance to realize what had happened. Mixed emotions filled us all as the realization of what had just happened sunk in. Lying before us was the king of kings in Alaska; a mature boar Alaskan brown bear which would square out at 8 foot 9 inches long, a bear with a rare blonde color phase, a bear that through five years of patience and persistence fulfilled a dream. The great Alaskan Brown Bear provided the desire to dream and the great state of Alaska had provided the backdrop of sights, sounds and experiences to make that dream come true. I would like to thank Rod and Lee for all the great memories. I look forward to pursuing the next DREAM.

I personally have not hunted bears in Alaska, but we have had some "brushes" with bears I want to tell you about.

BRUSHES WITH BEARS

With the exception of a couple of scary experiences, which you will soon hear about, in twenty-five years of hunting and some additional years fishing, we have never had a serious encounter with a bear. Nor have we ever lost any meat or fish to bears. This is not to say, however, that reasonable precautions and protection need not be taken. There are serious encounters between humans and bears every year in Alaska, and not only in Alaska. In Ontario, Canada, for example, the Ministry of Natural Resources has hired "bear-wise" specialists to field human-bear conflict calls twenty-fours hours a day during months when bears are not in hibernation. More that 10,000 calls have been received in a single year that require response by ministry personnel!

In Alaska, very few years go by without someone being killed or seriously mauled by a bear, and not just browns and grizzlies, blacks, too, can be a problem. A few years ago national publicity was given to the sad case of Timothy Treadwell, the man who chose to " live with bears", and his girl friend being killed and eaten. Records of confrontations with bears have been kept in Alaska since the late 1800s. In well over 100 years, only one person has been killed by a polar bear, five by blacks and fifty by browns or grizzlies.* About three times as many have been injured. But it just makes sense to not ask for trouble:

- Food should be kept in containers that will not leak odors. (And not in the tent where you sleep).

- Do not camp where bear are feeding on salmon.

- When bears are encountered, give them a wide birth.

- When walking through brushy areas, make plenty of noise. Take care not to surprise the animals.

- Pepper spray is a very effective deterrent. A loaded rifle is helpful but remember, it takes, on the average, four hits with a big game rifle to put down a brown or grizzly. Some guides prefer shotguns because they think they have more shocking power, but the downside is that the bear has to be awfully close to be effective. Some carry flare guns but the reports of how helpful they can be are mixed.

- Be especially careful when cubs are involved.

But nine times out of ten the bear will want to avoid you.

In this chapter you will read about our encounters with bears and I will also share stories I have heard first-hand from people in whom I have every confidence are telling the truth. Let me begin with the one encounter that had me genuinely concerned.

We had concluded a successful caribou hint with time to spare. Paul Carlson, our guide and outfitter, suggested that as long as the plane would not be in until the next day he would like to use our last afternoon trying to shoot a moose calf for meat for the winter. I volunteered to keep him company.

We took the ATV as far as we could go in the direction of the moose habitat but then found we would have to abandon the vehicle and go down through a gully to get closer to where Paul wanted to post. The gully wasn't really deep enough to be called a valley but it was full of thick alder brush and willows and some kinds of vegetation I couldn't identify. It would have been extremely difficult walking but we came across an animal trail that made the crossing fairly easy. At the bottom of the gully a tunnel

* 1883 to 2006

intersected our path. Paul explained that the tunnel was the result of animals passing that way for many years. It looked more like it had been carved out by a piece of heavy equipment. Paul said that it was generally believed that these tunnels were created by bears.

After negotiating the gully, we walked another half mile and then chose a hillside to sit on with a great view of the moose habitat. It was a great place to sit and visit but we only saw a cow and a calf way on the other side of the moose country and without the ATV, packing the meat would be difficult in the event we were successful.

After a couple of hours, we spotted a grizzly working his way along the hillside about 300 yards above us. He was obviously looking for food and stopped occasionally to dig in the tundra. When he was directly above us he stopped to dig out a ground squirrel. Every scoop of his paw sent a bushel of dirt flying - it was awesome! He finally seized the ground squirrel, sat back on his haunches and slowly chewed the little animal, tipping his head back to let the juices run down his throat.

When the bear had finished his meal, Paul suggested we head back to camp. To our surprise, the bear headed back along the hillside and seemed at the same time to be moving down hill, closer and closer to us. The 300 yards that separated us originally shrank to 200. I wasn't too concerned until Paul said, "That bear is stalking us!"

I should have explained earlier that I was carrying our only rifle. Paul had suggested when we left camp that I take my .300 because it was a bigger rifle in case of a long shot. Then, when Paul said, "I think you'd better let me carry the gun," I really became concerned.

When we came to the trail leading through the gully to our ATV, Paul directed, "You go ahead, I'll wait here until you are across. Once you are out of sight – run!"

By now the bear was less than 100 yards away.

I don't think I have ever moved faster, but when I reached the other side, I was relieved to see the bear just sitting where it was. When Paul saw I was out of the brush, he followed. To my immense relief, the bear did not move; he just sat there. And he was still sitting there when we drove out of sight on the ATV.

A side-note about the tunnels through the heavy brush. When Paul and I shared our experience with Chuck Crapechetts (Irene Carlson's teaching partner), he told me about an experience he had with these tunnels when guiding on a bear hunt. His client had wounded a grizzly that took off into some very heavy brush. Since he was the guide it was his job to go after the wounded animal. After giving the bear plenty of time to lie down and stiffen up, he went after it. He soon found one of these tunnels and blood droppings showed the bear was following it. Chuck came to a bend in the tunnel and as he rounded the corner he was confronted by the wounded grizzly, which was lying down but raised up when it saw Chuck. The bear was so close, Chuck just fired from the hip. Fortunately, the bear died instantly. Not a job for the fainthearted!

Vince Jarot, my dentist neighbor from Wadena, had at least an equally scary experience. Vince, Chet Snyder and I had walked over to the moose pasture one morning and for safety reasons had loaded our rifles but not put shells in the chambers. As we neared the river which ran through the moose habitat, Vince announced that he would cross the stream. Chet and I decided to hunt this side. Vince took off and Chet and I continued to visit, giving our partner time to get across the river.

Vince had been gone only a few minutes when he returned, with eyes as big as saucers and hyperventilating. He was unable to talk for a couple of minutes, but when he was able to speak, this is what he shared:

"After I left you guys I came to a little valley in the tundra between here and the river. As I reached the bottom of the valley, two brown bears appeared just above me and headed right towards me. I just froze. I couldn't move. I thought about my rifle but I remembered I didn't have a shell in the chamber, but I just couldn't move to throw one in. The bears kept coming and passed me, one on either side - totally ignoring me!"

Many questions later, the three of us mounted the nearest hill to see if we could see the bears, but they were nowhere in sight. But what an experience!

Next I would like to share my own near-bear experience.

I was hunting alone and making an effort to sneak on a distant small herd of caribou. I had been using a small grove of brush and trees to hide me as I worked my way in their direction. When I peeked around a stand of heavy foliage, I was shocked to see the huge rear end of a brown bear just twenty or thirty paces in front of me! The bear was feeding on blueberries and with the wind in my face he was totally oblivious to my presence. I lost no time in backing up behind the trees and brush, never taking my eyes off the bear. I quickly put as much distance as possible between me and the huge animal, and never saw it again. It is interesting that I can't remember whether or not I ever had a shot at the caribou, but I can remember every detail of my encounter with the bear.

Bears love berries and in late August and September there are tons of them on the tundra. Bears seem to be especially fond of blueberries which seem to have a laxative effect on the animals. The result is huge, cow-pie like droppings along the trails that look all too much like blueberry pies. After encountering these pies in my earlier years of hunting in Alaska I lost all desire to eat blueberry pie. Fortunately, I did get over it.

I referred to this particular bear as a "brown bear", and it was. There have been countless arguments over the years as to which bears are brown bears and which are grizzlies. The truth is, they are the same species. Brown bears tend to live closer to salt water, however, and to grow a little bigger than grizzlies, maybe because they eat more fish. Grizzlies then tend to be found more inland and are a variety of colors, including black with silver tips, cream colored, light blue tint, etc. Both are usually bigger than black bears. The Kodiak browns are the biggest of all; the record being slightly over 1400 pounds. Typical male browns on the mainland tend to be less than half that and females smaller yet.

Gordy Dezell, one of our hunters, also had an experience with a bear that was nearly as close as my encounter. I had just crossed a wide but shallow stream and was waiting for Gordy on the far side and had an excellent view of the incident. Although the stream was shallow it was also very swift and crossing it was not easy. There was a bend in the river a couple hundred yards upstream, and as Gordy neared the middle, a brown bear came around the bend chasing a salmon! I was afraid Gordy hadn't seen the bear and was about to fire a warning shot when Gordy looked to his right, and raised his rifle. I thought he would fire any second. But when the bear was within a hundred yards the salmon reversed field and headed back upstream, with the bear right behind him. Soon he was out of sight.

I asked Gordy later if he had an action plan. He replied that in another few seconds he would have fired in front of the bear and if that didn't stop him his next shot would be directly at the animal.

On one trip we, unfortunately, met a woman, briefly, who had just experienced a terrible tragedy involving a bear. She and her husband visited the Iliamna area most every year and stayed with Paul and Irene Carlson in their lodge before and after their fishing ventures. This particular year they had a float plane drop them off on a nameless small lake which had excellent rainbow and "dolly" fishing. The first day, the husband announced that he would like to walk around the relatively small body of water to where a stream entered the lake, to catch some fish for lunch. He left the rifle they had brought along for protection with his wife and took off.

After he had been fishing for awhile, the wife picked up the rifle to look through the scope to see how her husband was doing. At that moment, a bear came out of the brush behind the fisherman and appeared to attack him. She dropped the rifle and screamed. When she looked again, the bear was gone but her husband was lying on the ground. When she reached him, she found he was dead! The plane wasn't due back for three days and she was thus left all alone in this horrible situation.

We flew into Iliamna the same day she flew out.

Paul and Irene learned later that the autopsy determined that the man had died of a heart attack. There were no puncture wounds but they could not tell whether or not the bear had struck the man or if the heart attack was totally the result of shear fright.

I heard first hand of another scary encounter a hunter had with a bear. We were in the Iliamna airport waiting for a plane to take us back to Anchorage, when a hunter came limping in. After submitting his ticket at the reservation desk, he hobbled over to where we were sitting and took a seat across from me. He was obviously a hunter and I asked if he had been hurt while hunting.

He replied, "You might say that. Actually, I was chewed on by a bear!"

All eyes were instantly on the hunter as we urged him to tell us the story.

He began by carefully pulling up his pants leg, revealing a heavily bandaged area between his ankle and his knee. He went on, "I had been hunting with my guide and his wife and we were staying in their cabin. We hadn't even seen a bear. After a few days the guide decided to fly back to Iliamna for some more provisions. He hadn't been gone long when his wife decided to wash some clothes, which she then went outside to hang up. It was a beautiful day, so I decided to sit outside and keep her company. Like a fool, I didn't take my rifle with me. All of a sudden a bear came into the clearing. We both hollered and yelled but he just kept walking slowly towards us. The guide's wife suddenly took off running for the cabin. I figured I'd better do the same, but she had a head start and got there first, went into the cabin and slammed the door in my face! Somehow the door locked and as I was screaming for her to open up I felt the bear grab my leg. I was hanging onto the doorknob for dear life and the bear was tugging and chewing on my leg. Luckily, my boots gave me some protection. Just as she got the door open the bear let go just long enough for me to get inside and slam the door in the bear's face. The guide's wife was standing there with her husband's rifle – prepared to shoot if the bear tried to come in.

We were too excited to think about opening a window and shooting the bear, which finally wandered off as casually as it had come. And that was the only bear we saw in the entire trip."

After one of our close-encounter experiences I asked Paul Carlson if he had any stories to share.

"Actually," Paul responded, "I've only had one experience that rivaled our being stalked by that grizzly when we were looking for a calf moose. I was guiding a guy on a bear hunt. We had seen a couple of smaller animals but he wanted a trophy or nothing. On the third day of our hunt we returned to camp to find our tent badly torn and our ATV missing. It didn't take long to locate the 4-wheeler but we were surprised to find a chunk taken out of one of the tires and the seat ripped open. It had been dragged a couple of hundred yards by a bear!

We slept in the tent that night, luckily, it didn't rain. In the middle of the night we were awakened by the bear rubbing against the tent. It was a bright, moon-lit night and I was able to see a big paw come through the tear in the tent and brush within inches of my nose! I said the dumbest thing. I said, who - who - who's there??? I knew darn well who was there! It was the bear of course.

But by speaking I apparently spooked the bear which then backed off. When my hunter and I looked through the opening in the tent we saw this big brownie sitting in the moon light about twenty yards from the tent, looking in our direction.

Shooting a bear at night is not legal, but I was so mad at that bear and concerned that we wouldn't find another that big - it truly was trophy size - that I asked my client if he wanted to shoot it. To my surprise he said no, he wanted everything legal. In retrospect, I can't believe I said it, but I further encouraged him to shoot by pointing out that the bear had harassed us and we were in danger. But again he said he'd take his chances and would only shoot if it attacked us. So then I began hollering at the bear, thinking it might be provoked to come toward us, but the bear just got up and slowly walked away."

"So did your client ever get a bear that trip?" I asked.

"No," Paul replied. "We never even saw a bear after that."

One of us then asked Paul if he had any other bear stories to share.

"Not really," he said, "but a fishing guide friend of mine had quite an experience this past summer. He and his party had spent the morning fishing a stream that runs into Lake Iliamna, and had walked out to the lake where they had left their boat to have lunch. After lunch, Fred, that's the guide's name, suggested the fishermen work their way back upstream and he would clean-up and join them shortly. When he had finished cleaning up, he decided to take a short-cut through the brush rather than wade up the river. About half-way there, he was stepping over a fallen tree and almost stepped on a sleeping bear. The bear came to and quickly stood up on its hind legs, literally looking down into the guide's face! Fred said he had a revolver on his hip but absolutely couldn't move. The bear said "Wuff", then dropped down and walked away!"

Nearly all of these big game recipes were collected and/or originated in Alaska and were designed for moose and caribou. You will find, however, that they will work well with any big game, or for domestic meats for that matter.

You will note that you are cautioned to trim away the fat on any wild game; this is very important. The exception is caribou, which carry their fat on their backs where it is not a problem.

STEAKS

BROILED
– Use thick cuts (3/4 inch to 1 inch)

– Trim away all fat.

– Broil on the grill or under the broiler in your stove. When the steak is well-browned, turn it over. The degree of doneness depends, of course, on two factors: heat and time. Because everyone has his own preference (rare, medium rare, medium, well done, etc.) and because the heat will vary with the stove or grill, there is no time formula; but for a starter, try 5 minutes on a side. You will have to learn by experience and will probably end up testing with a knife until you've done a hundred or more – outside appearances of a steak are deceiving. Just remember: The more you cut meat, the more juice you lose.

– Generally speaking – the hotter the broiler the better.

– Place the orders for "well done" on first and the orders for rare on last so that the steaks will all be ready at the same time.

– Serve on a hot platter.

FRIED

- Use thick cuts.
- Trim off the fat.
- Preheat the pan or griddle until almost "smoking hot" - use a light coat of oil.
- Fry on both sides to the degree of "doneness" ordered by your guests. Again, until you have the experience, you will probably have to test with your knife (the more you cut meat, the more juice you lose) by making a small cut on one edge. Place the orders for "well done" on first and "rare" on last.
- Season and serve on a hot platter. Seasoning steaks before or as you fry them tends to make them tougher.

BAKED STEAK

- Bake only tougher cuts of meat. Save you choice, tender cuts for broiling or frying.
- Use 1/2 to 3/4 inch steaks. (trim off fat.)

MUSHROOM STYLE

- Arrange the steaks in a single layer in a baking dish or oven pan. A skillet will do, providing it does not have a wood or plastic handle. Season lightly with salt and pepper.
- Cover the steaks with mushroom soup. One 26 oz. can of soup plus one can of water will cover two pounds of steaks. Be sure the liquid covers the meat. Add a can of mushroom pieces and parts.
- Cover the pan or dish. If you do not have a cover that fits, use foil.
- Place in preheated 300° oven. Bake for two hours, or use a crockpot for at least five hours.

SWISS STEAK (Tomato Style)

– 2 pounds round steak (trim away fat)

– 1 26 oz. can tomato soup

– 1 can water

– 1 cup chopped celery

– 1 large sliced onion

– 1 small, sliced green pepper

– salt and pepper

– Season steaks and arrange in single layer in baking dish or pan.

– Add chopped celery, sliced onion, and sliced green pepper.

– Cover with soup mixture (tomato soup and equal amount of water). Be sure meat is covered by liquid.

– Place in preheated, 300° oven and bake for two hours, or use a crockpot and cook for at least five hours.

– Serve baked steaks with boiled, baked, or mashed potatoes. The liquid may be used as a gravy. A salad and vegetable will complete the meal.

BAKED STEAK WITH ONION SOUP MIX

– Use 1/2 to 3/4 inch cuts. Trim away any fat.

– Lay steaks on foil. Place generous pats of margarine or butter here and there on steaks; about one quarter pound in all for 2 pounds of steak.

– Sprinkle one envelope of dry onion soup mix over two pounds of steaks – evenly.

– Bring the foil over the steaks and seal on top.

– Place in preheated 250° oven for two hours or use a crockpot for five hours.

– Serve with potatoes, salad, and vegetable. The onion soup mix may be poured into a bowl and mixed with an equal amount of hot water – then used as a gravy or poured over the steaks – or both.

– This is an excellent way to prepare steaks that have been in your freezer several months (even a year). But first trim off any freezer "burn."

SOUTH SEAS MARINATED STEAK
– Two pounds of steaks - 3/4 to 1 inch thick. Trim off fat.

– Marinating Sauce

– 1/2 cup salad oil

– 2 tablespoons soy sauce

– 1/4 cup sugar

– 1/4 cup finely chopped onion

– 1/2 tablespoon salt, 1/2 tablespoon pepper

– 4 tablespoons sesame seed

– Place steaks in a shallow dish or pan. Cover with marinade.

– Let stand overnight in refrigerator.

– If the sauce does not cover the steaks, brush surface generously and then turn the steaks over in the morning.

– Broil the steaks. Baste with sauce.

TENDERIZED STEAK (Cube Steak)
Even the more choice cuts of wild game can sometimes be tough. Here is one way to make them more "chewable" without sacrificing the flavor.

– Sprinkle a liberal portion of flour over each steak and vigorously pound it into the meat. Ideally, you should use a mallet designed for the job, however, the butt end of your hunting knife will do the trick. Turn the steaks over and repeat.

– Now broil them on a hot grill or fry them in a hot pan lightly coated with oil. The steaks will get done quickly – about four or five minutes to the side.

TENDERIZING MEATS

There are a number of meat tenderizing powders on the market which work quickly and do a good job, but they may change the flavor somewhat.

A better method – but more time consuming – is to marinate the meat.

– 1 cup white vinegar (or cooking wine or sherry)

– 1 cup water

– 10 whole cloves

– 6 bay leaves

– 1 tablespoon whole black peppers

– 1 large onion, chopped

– Marinate steaks for at least 24 hours; up to three days for a roast. Keep under refrigeration. Turn steaks or roast every 12 hours.

– If you make more than two cups of marinade, use proportionately more spices.

– If you don't have time to marinate a wild game roast, rubbing with a solution of half water and half vinegar will help eliminate distracting flavors.

BAKED CHOPS

– Use thick or "double chops". Trim away the fat.

– Season the chops, then brown both sides. Prepare your favorite stuffing.

– Place the stuffing in a baking dish or roaster.

– "Submerge" the chops in the dressing.

– Cover and place in a preheated 300° oven for 1-1/2 hours. Be sure the chops are tender and well done – all the way through.

– Serve with salad, baked potatoes, and a vegetable.

ROASTS

Good Quality or Tender Roasts – such as Rib, Tenderloin or Rump

– Remove fat.

– Rub roast with salt, pepper, and garlic salt.

– Place on a rack in a shallow pan. Lay a couple of pieces of fat bacon on top.

– Leave pan uncovered; do not add water.

– Place in preheated medium oven (320-325°).

– Allow
  – 28-30 minutes per pound for rare
  – 32-35 minutes per pound for medium
  – 37-40 minutes per pound for well done.

It is a good idea to use a thermometer. It is easy to spoil a roast by having it either too well done or undercooked in the center.

– A meat thermometer will read:
  – 140° for rare
  – 160° for medium
  – 170° for well done

Baked potatoes, squash, and corn go well with a roast.

POT ROASTS

Use with tougher cuts of Wild Game

– Trim fat from the roast.

– Rub in salt and pepper - you may also want to try garlic salt.

– Roll the roast in flour and brown all sides in cooking oil.

– Add one-half cup of water, cover tightly, and cook slowly for two and one-half to three hours (275° to 300° oven), or use a crockpot for at least five hours.

– For a true pot roast dinner, add whole small onions, carrots, and whole, peeled small potatoes the last hour.

ALL PURPOSE GRAVY RECIPE

– After you remove the roast, skim any fat from the remaining meat stock.

– Using a covered pint jar for a shaker, add 1/2 cup of water and 1/4 cup of flour. Shake until well mixed. If you don't have a jar, use any small container. Place the flour in the container and add a little water. Using a spoon, make a smooth paste. Now add the balance of the water and stir until well blended - no lumps.

– Remove the stock from the heat and slowly stir in the flour and water mixture. Return to the stove and simmer, meanwhile stirring constantly. When the gravy is bubbling all over in the pan, add a tablespoon of Kitchen Bouquet. add salt and pepper; continue to stir for another five minutes. Serve.

STEW

Since it takes so long to prepare a stew "from scratch," we are going to cheat a little! We will use canned beef stew as a base and a roast instead of regular stew meat. There just isn't enough meat in most canned stews to satisfy a hungry man.

Four servings:

– 2 cans of beef stew (24 oz. cans)

– 1 can mixed vegetables (#2 can)

– 1 large can tomato soup (26 oz. can)

– 1-1/2 to 2 pounds of pre-cooked wild game roast, cut into bite-size portions. (Leftover roast makes great stew meat)

– Empty the contents of the cans of beef stew, mixed vegetables and tomato soup into an iron kettle or deep iron skillet. stir in precooked meat chunks.

– Simmer on top of the stove for 40 minutes; stir occasionally.

SPAGHETTI

SAUCE:
– Start the sauce first.
– Brown 1-1/2 lb. wild game hamburger
– Add one small can tomato paste and one can water and simmer 15 minutes.
– In a separate pan, brown one large onion (chopped) and 1 cup chopped celery.
– Add the onion and celery to the hamburger-tomato mixture. Also add 2 cans
    tomato soup, 1/2 tsp. allspice, 1/2 tsp. ginger, 1 tsp. chili powder, and a least 1 tbsp.
    worcestershire sauce (more if you like it spicy). Simmer mixture for another
    15 min. and serve over spaghetti.

SPAGHETTI:
Use about 14 oz. of long spaghetti (average size package) to serve four. Drop the spaghetti into three quarts of rapidly boiling water to which two tablespoons (level) of salt have been added. A little butter or cooking oil will keep the spaghetti from sticking together. Let boil for about five or six minutes and then drain through a colander (a sieve like utensil made of metal or plastic). If you don't have a sieve, use a cover to hold the spaghetti in the kettle and pour off all the water. Rinse the spaghetti thoroughly with hot water to prevent a "starchy" taste. Now add a chunk of butter or margarine (about 1/8 pound - half a stick) to the hot spaghetti and stir gently. Place the spaghetti and sauce in separate bowls and let each guest serve himself.

SAUCES FOR USE WITH BIG GAME

BORDELAISE SAUCE
Use with big game cuts.
Ingredients for 3 pounds of steaks, chops or a small roast:
– 3 T butter
– 3 T cornstarch
– 1 can consommé
– 1/2 can (3/4 cup) red wine
– Melt butter in saucepan; add cornstarch and blend. Stir in consommé and wine.
    Cook over low heat; whisk frequently to keep sauce smooth. Will need to be
    thinned if reheated. Makes about 2 1/4 cups.

GRAPE HOT SAUCE

May be served over either big game cuts or with ducks.

Ingredients for 2 ducks or 4 pounds of steaks or chops:
– 4 T butter, melted
– 1/2 cup chopped onion or green onions
– 1/2 cup grape jelly (other tart jellies may be substituted)
– 1 cup red wine
– 1/4 t Tabasco sauce
– Sauté onion in 1 T butter. Stir in all other ingredients, adding the remainder of the butter last, one spoon at a time. Continue heating and stirring until the sauce thickens.

PRUNE SAUCE

This sauce will add a delightful flavor to ducks, geese or sliced roast.

Ingredients for about 4 pounds of meat:
– 1/2 cup prune juice
– 1/2 cup white wine
– 1/2 cup water
– 1 T flour
– 1/2 bouillon cube
– Begin by combining the wine and flour in a saucepan over low heat. Gradually stir in all other ingredients and continue stirring and cooking until sauce thickens. Serve hot over meat.

CIDER SAUCE

Serve over chops or steaks.

Ingredients for 1 1/2 pounds of steaks or chops:
– 1 T butter
– 1 large, hard, red apple – peeled and chopped
– 1 small chopped onion
– 1/2 cup cider
– salt and pepper to taste
– Melt the butter and sauté the apple and onion a few minutes until tender. Add cider; continue to cook and stir until the sauce thickens. Serve over steaks or chops.

SPICY MUSTARD SAUCE

– 1 cup mustard

– 2 T horseradish

– 2 T vinegar

– 2 T honey

– 2 drops Tabasco sauce

– Blend all ingredients.

HONEY-MUSTARD SEASONING

– 1/2 cup mustard

– 1/2 cup honey

– 6 T mayonnaise or yogurt or half of each

– Blend all ingredients.

HONEY-MUSTARD SAUCE

Serve over big game steaks

Ingredients for 2 pounds of meat:

– 1 T butter or oil

– 3 T flour

– 2 T honey

– 2 T mustard

– 3/4 cup beef or chicken broth

– 1 T lemon juice

– 1/2 cup red wine

– 1 T chopped chives or parsley for garnish

– Melt butter; stir in flour; cook 1 minute; add wine and broth - continue stirring. Add mustard, honey and lemon juice. Continue to heat and stir until the sauce thickens. Serve hot over steaks; garnish with chopped chives or parsley.

HONEY-GARLIC SAUCE

Serve over chops or steaks. May be used as a marinade with tougher cuts.

Ingredients for about 2 pounds of meat:

– 2 T minced garlic

– 5 T honey

– 4 T sherry

– 3 T lemon juice

– 3 T soy sauce

– Combine all ingredients and heat until bubbly.

– If used as a marinade, save for basting and/or to be served with the meat.

COCKTAIL SAUCE FOR MEATBALLS

Prepare miniature meatballs from 2 pounds of big game hamburger using your favorite recipe. Serve with the following sauce:

Ingredients:

– 1 bottle chili sauce

– 1 pint jar currant jelly (or other tart jelly)

– 2 lemons, juiced

– 3 T horseradish

– Combine all ingredients and serve hot as a dip for pre-cooked meatballs.

TOMATO SAUCE OVER MEATBALLS

Prepare meatballs from 1 1/4 pounds of big game hamburger using your favorite recipe. Set meatballs side-by-side in a baking dish and top with the following recipe. Bake in a medium oven until well done. Check after 40 minutes.

Sauce ingredients:

– 1 can tomato puree (large)

– 1/2 cup water

– 2 T minced garlic

– 4 drops Tabasco sauce

– 2 T brown sugar

– 1 T oregano, chopped

– 2 T parsley, chopped

– Combine all ingredients and brush on or pour carefully over meatballs. Bake.

PINEAPPLE MEATBALL SAUCE

Prepare meatballs from about 2 pounds of big game hamburger using your favorite recipe. Bake the meatballs in the following sauce:

Ingredients:

– 2 14 oz. cans crushed pineapple

– 2 cups brown sugar

– 3 T mustard

– 2 T vinegar

– 1 T soy sauce

Combine all ingredients in a baking dish. Place meatballs in the sauce. Bake in medium oven, covered, until well done. Test after 40 minutes.

SOUR CREAM-DILL SAUCE

Dill sauce is usually associated with fish, but this sauce works well with steaks or chops. It may also be poured over big game meatballs.

Ingredients for about 2 pounds of meat:

– 2 cups beef broth

– 2 T minced dill

– 1 cup sour cream

– 1/4 cup flour

– 1/8 t pepper

– 1/8 t nutmeg

– 2 T capers

– 1/4 pound butter melted

– Combine the melted butter, broth and flour. Stir until smooth. Heat until bubbly, stirring all the time. Add sour cream, dill, capers, pepper and nutmeg. Stir and continue heating until it starts to boil. Remove from heat and serve over prepared steaks, chops or meatballs.

BARBECUE SAUCE #1

Excellent with ribs.

Ingredients to flavor about 6 pounds of ribs:

- 2 T butter, melted
- 2 T chopped onion
- 2 T minced garlic
- 1 cup red wine vinegar
- 1/2 cup brown sugar
- 2 cups catsup
- 2 cups chili sauce
- 1 T liquid smoke
- 4 drops Tabasco sauce
- Sauté the onion and garlic in the melted butter. Combine sugar and vinegar, heat until it is about half the original volume. Combine all ingredients and blend thoroughly. If time permits, let refrigerate a few hours so that the flavors blend well.

BARBECUE SAUCE #2

Ingredients for about 3 pounds of ribs:

- 1 cup catsup
- 1/2 cup red vinegar
- 2 T Worcestershire sauce
- 2 T sugar
- 1 t salt
- 1/4 cup water
- 6 drops Tabasco sauce (adjust to taste)
- 1 T celery seed
- Combine all ingredients in a saucepan. Simmer until liquid is reduced to 2/3 original volume.

MUSHROOM SAUCES

MEXICAN MUSHROOM SAUCE

A multi-purpose sauce that may be served over big game steaks or roasts. Steaks may also be baked in this sauce.

Ingredients for about 4 pounds of meat:

– 3 cups fresh mushrooms (sliced or whole)

– 1 can tomato sauce (If you use Mexican variety, reduce or eliminate chili powder.)

– 1 can tomato puree

– 1 green pepper, chopped

– 1 small onion, chopped

– 1 T chili powder

– 1/4 pound butter

– Sauté mushrooms, green pepper and onion in butter until tender.

– Add all other ingredients and simmer 1 hour. Add the sauce during the last 10 minutes of preparation and serve over meat.

CREAMY MUSHROOM SAUCE

May be served over will game steaks or roasts.

Ingredients for about 3 pounds of meat:

– 1 pound fresh mushrooms (preferably wild)

– 1/4 pound butter (1 stick)

– 1 cup heavy cream

– 2 T chopped parsley

– salt and pepper to taste

– If mushrooms are small, use whole, otherwise slice. Sauté the mushrooms in the butter 3 or 4 minutes until tender. Add the cream. Continue heating until bubbly. Season lightly with salt and pepper. Sprinkle parsley on top.

MUSHROOM SAUCES (For Roasting or Broiling)

SAUCE NUMBER ONE

Ingredients for about 3 pounds of meat:
- 1 cup fresh mushrooms, sliced
- 1 cup sour cream
- 1/8 pound butter (1/2 stick)
- 3 T flour
- 1/2 cup milk
- 1/2 T Worcestershire sauce
- salt and pepper to taste
- Sauté the mushrooms in the melted butter. Stir in all other ingredients (except salt and pepper), adding the sour cream last. Cook until sauce starts to thicken (stirring regularly). Stir in salt and pepper to taste. serve over steaks or roasts.

SAUCE NUMBER TWO

Ingredients for about 4 pounds of meat:
- 2 cups fresh mushrooms, sliced (If canned mushrooms are substituted, use about half the volume.)
- 1 can tomato sauce
- 1 can tomato puree
- 1 small green pepper, chopped
- 1 small onion, chopped
- 1/4 pound butter (1 stick) melted
- Sauté the mushrooms in the melted butter. Stir in all other ingredients and simmer for one hour, stirring occasionally. Serve over steaks or roasts.

SPICY MUSHROOM SAUCE

Serve over most any cut of big game.

Ingredients for 2 pounds of cuts:
- 1 T butter, melted
- 1 cup mushroom pieces (preferably wild)
- 2 T minced garlic
- 1/2 cup white wine
- 1/2 cup beef or chicken broth
- 1 1/2 t fresh ground black pepper
- Sauté the garlic in the melted butter about 1 minute. Add mushroom pieces and cook until tender (about 2 minutes). Add remaining ingredients and continue to cook and stir until the sauce thickens. Serve hot over meat.

PART II
FISHING IN ALASKA

Chapter 6
FISHING ADVENTURES

Greg Liefermann (Staples, MN) with the biggest Silver Salmon any of our group has ever caught (18 1/2" pounds). This one came from the Kenai River.

My friend, Ed Morey*, and his wife, Dolores, had just returned from fishing in Alaska and he called to say. "We've got to have lunch. I have so much to tell you about our fishing trip."

I had fished lake trout with Ed in northern Canada and eastern brook trout in Labrador. On several Alaskan big game hunting trips we had fished together for rainbows and Dolly Vardens, but I had never heard Ed so excited about fishing. Needless to say, we had lunch at our first opportunity.

Ed began by raving about the king salmon he and Dolores had caught – several over 40 pounds. He said several times, "You just can't believe how powerful they are."

Ed said that he and Dolores had a guide, Chick Kishbaugh, of Soldotna. He explained that a guide was necessary, especially for the beginner, because the Kenai River was so fast – about 10 miles an hour – and had many hidden bars and rocks. Also, he added that the kings hung out in holes, usually well out into the river.

Ed then changed the discussion to sockeyes (reds). He said that the sockeyes hung out closer to shore in the slower current and could be fished with waders. He said they ran between four and ten pounds and were great fighters, sometimes jumping clear out of the water. Ed added that they had been fortunate in being up there during the fairly brief sockeye run up the river to spawn, only about two or three weeks of hot fishing. They had gone to Alaska for the kings, so the reds were sort of a bonus fish. The king season ran from May to the end of July on the Kenai.

The fishing had not been limited to the Kenai. The Kasilof River was only about twenty miles from Soldotna and offered quite a different experience of fishing for kings. Whereas the Kenai was heavily fished with outboard motor driven boats, motors were not allowed on the Kasilof, only drift boats propelled by oars, manned by guides. Whereas the Kenai could be very noisy and extremely busy during the sockeye run, the Kasilof was very quiet and more of a wilderness experience. Although the kings in the Kasilof did not run as large as those on the Kenai, they had plenty of fight and fishing them from a drift boat added to the excitement.

When Ed had finished raving about the salmon fishing, he added, "And then we had a day of halibut fishing on the Ocean. That was sort of icing on the cake!"

* Founder of the Morey Fish Company, Motley, MN.

He went on to tell about catching the huge slabs. Their biggest was nearly 70 pounds. And of course they are among the best eating fish that swim.

As you can well imagine, we had a very long lunch, but when it was over, I just knew I had to give salmon fishing a try the next summer. The many successful big game hunting trips had helped me fall in love with Alaska; Ed's enthusiasm gave me a whole different opportunity (or excuse!) to enjoy this great state.

CHAD LONGBELLA AND I HEAD FOR ALASKA

And so it was that in July of that next year, Chad Longbella and I headed for Alaska. Yes, just the two of us. The guys who had been hunting in previous years wanted to do that again in the fall and for family or business reasons felt they couldn't make both trips. But our experience that summer, along with Ed Morey's stories, was the beginning of expeditions of Minnesotans every summer (and they are still continuing) to the Kenai Peninsula to fish salmon and halibut. Some years there have been two trips, one in July for kings and reds and another in August for silvers. Personally, I have fished tuna and marlin in the Sea of Cortez (Mexico), tarpon off the shores of Costa Rica, lake trout in the Northwest territory and muskies in Ontario, and as great as those experiences have been, none of them equal salmon fishing in Alaska.

But back to the story of our first trip. Based on the Morey's experience, Chad and I chose the third week of July for our trip, so that we could fish both sockeyes (reds) and kings. We also contacted Chick Kishbaugh, the guide the Moreys had raved so much about. We flew into Anchorage, rented a car and made the three hour trip to Soldotna. (In more recent years we have been flying into the Kenai airport and rented cars there.) Chick had arranged for us to stay in the walkout basement apartment of Paul and Nancy Gray, and we have been staying there every summer since. It is located right on the Kenai River and we have had great success fishing reds right in front of their house.

Chick keeps his boat about a five minute drive from Grays, and we met him there at the crack of dawn that next morning. His younger son, Adam, an eighth grader, came along as helper. If I learned one thing about fishing kings, it is that I would have been better off if I had never fished before. As I mentioned earlier, the Kenai is a very swift river (about 10 miles an hour). We began fishing right out in front of where Chick keeps his boat. He nosed his boat into the current and left it in forward gear, but slow enough so that the boat slowly slipped down stream. He instructed Chad and me to let our line out seven complete runs of the level winder on the reels. (This would vary a little depending on how deep the hole was.)

For lures, Chick used a Quickfish*– a shiny, metal lure to which Chick tied two fillets of sardines - one to each side. Several feet in front of the lure was a plastic diver which got the lure down near the bottom.

We were instructed to either hold the rod in our laps or place it in a rod holder. I have learned over the years that I am better off putting my rod in the holder so that I don't try to set the hook too soon. Chick advised us to not set the hook until he said to and that as we set the hook, he would gun the motor forward to help penetrate the tough mouths of the kings.

Chad had the first strike and did everything right. After the first few minutes of the fight, Chick positioned the boat downstream from the salmon so that Chad wouldn't be fighting the current. We must have drifted at least a mile before we even saw the fish. We probably drifted another quarter mile before Chick slipped the net under the salmon - a bright silver 30 pounder. We were only allowed to keep two kings, but Chad opted to put this one in the box.

I had the next two strikes, but both times made the mistake of putting my thumb on the reel as I set the hook. Both times I broke the fifty pound test line we were using.

I was just too accustomed to catching walleyes! There was a ballpean hammer lying in the tray next to Chick. After I broke the line for the second time, Chick picked up the hammer and said, "If you put your thumb on the reel next time you get a strike, I'm going to hit it with this hammer!"

It turned out, those were the only two strikes I had that first day.

The second day we went several miles downstream where we tried an entirely different technique - called "bouncing eggs." Chick had kept the eggs from each female that was caught and treated them with a special substance available at bait shops which "cured" the eggs and toughened them. The eggs were then held on the single hook by a loop in the line. The current was a little slower down stream and as the name of the technique implies, we just bounced them along the bottom. Again, when we had a bite,

*Chick also uses a large version of the flatfish lure.

Chad's 55 pound kind salmon. It is on display in Longbella's Drug Stores, Staples, MN.

Chick would tells us when to set the hook. I finally landed my first king – and it was a dandy – over 40 pounds. To add to the excitement, it dove under the boat and then jumped completely out of the water on the other side. I'll have to admit, without Chick's coaching I probably would never have landed it. The fish was so powerful there was no way I could simply reel it in. After I had been fighting it for over a half-hour, it seemed to "sound" below the boat. Chick instructed, "Reel down – lift up; reel down – lift up."

When I finally had it on the surface, I said, "I think it's ready to net."

Chick answered firmly, "I'll tell you when it's ready to net!"

In due time, Chick finally ordered, "reel down to the diver and slowly lift up."

Chick just doesn't miss with the net, and my first king went into the box.

And speaking of our guide, I should say a few words about Chick. He is a transplanted Pennsylvanian and a former elementary teacher. He is probably unique as a guide in that he has a bachelor's degree and two master degrees – one in environmental education. This knowledge comes in handy in that his clients (or as he calls them

–"patients") have a million questions about fish, game and the environment. He also has a million stories. If you spend the whole week in his boat you might just hear some of them twice. On this first trip, Adam drove his dad crazy. Every time Chick would pause in telling a story, Adam would quickly jump in and finish it. He knew them all! For several years now, Adam has been his dad's partner and does a great job in his own right. An older son, Matt, has also done some guiding but now works as a surveyor. I really miss Matt. He captained a drift boat and I always looked forward to spending at least one day with him. Chick and Adam now have a select few guides who work with them. I never worry if I don't have Chick or Adam; they are all excellent or they don't work long for the Kishbaughs.

Back to our story. Chad and I each caught another "keeper". Chad's was a bright chrome 55 pounder just in from the sea. My second fish was a little larger than my first. Chad's trophy is mounted on the wall of the Longbella Drug Store in Staples.

Now lets talk about sockeyes or "reds" as most Alaskans call them. They are my favorite salmon, not just because they are good fighters and fun to catch, but because they taste so darn good. We usually smoke the kings because they are more oily and for that reason smoke better. We keep them refrigerated while in Alaska but just shrink wrap them and pack them with our other luggage when we go home. Since they are smoked, they will not spoil in that short a time. The weight we are allowed for a

The author with his larger King and some of the Sockeyes (Reds) Adam helped him catch.

cooler is limited, so we use that entirely for reds and halibut – both of which we shrink wrap in serving size portions and then freeze. They will stay frozen during the relatively short flight home.

I would guess the sock eyes are called "reds" because their meat is the most red of all salmon. It is also true that once they have entered freshwater they begin to lose their chrome appearance and gradually turn red by the time they spawn, but other salmon do that too. As salmon turn red their flesh softens, but they are still tasty.

Now, back to Chad and my first Alaska salmon fishing experience. We tried for reds in front of Grays, where we were staying, but only caught a couple and I know now we hooked them by accident. So, the day Chad and I each put a king "in the box" and therefore had to quit fishing them, we asked Chick to show us how to catch sockeyes. As it turned out, Adam became our teacher.

Chick dropped us off on a sandbar where others were already fishing. Adam explained that reds, unlike other varieties of salmon, stop feeding when they leave the salt water and start their trip upstream to spawn. Also, unlike the kings, they stay in the shallower water near shore and therefore there is no point in casting out more than about fifteen feet. He further explained that the reds move quite slowly up stream in schools and often just hold themselves still in the current. Since they aren't feeding, they would be impossible to catch except that they have a habit of constantly opening and closing their mouths.

Adam outfitted our fairly long and limber spinning rods with a single hook, as the law requires, and a couple of splitshot to keep the line close to the bottom. The hook had feathers tied to it, but since the reds were not interested in eating, they were purely for decoration. He then instructed us to flip the lure out about 15 feet and then follow the line with the tip of the rod as the "lure" drifted with the current. In other words, the line should be kept straight out from the end of the rod. He added, "If you see the line or end of the rod twitch, even the tiniest bit, or feel anything, set the hook – hard. Hopefully the line will be in the salmon's mouth and when you set the hook that will then sink it into the fish's mouth. If you snag a fish anyplace except in the mouth, you have to release it."

And so Chad and I began casting and retrieving but with no action – cast after cast. Finally, Adam grabbed my rod and on his very first cast, set the hook and the water exploded as a 10 pound sockeye took to the air! He then handed me the rod, saying, "That's how it's done!"

Don Hester (Cass Lake, MN) and his 35 pound Halibut.

He cautioned me not to let it get out into the fast water because I'd probably never get it back in. After about ten minutes of shear fun, Adam netted the fish.

Then Adam turned to Chad and said, "Let me see your rod."

On the third or fourth cast Adam again set the hook and handed the rod back to Chad. The fish wasn't quite as big as mine but was an equally good fighter. Chad was also successful in bringing it to Adam's net.

For the next hour or so, Adam alternated between the two of us as the action continued. I'm sure the other fishermen had a good laugh at our expense as they watched this eighth grader help us catch our fish. Several times, Chad or I tried it on our own but to no avail. Later in the trip with lots of practice, we finally learned the system. But even now, after years of fishing sockeyes, I know I'm not as good as Adam was then when he was just a young kid - and he hasn't lost his touch!

When one has an experience like Chad and I had on our first purely for fishing Alaskan adventure, every little detail is imbedded in your mind. The many other trips since sort of blend together, but that first experience will always be special. Since then, I have caught bigger kings – like the 70 pounder I caught a couple of years ago - and I don't have any idea how many reds I've caught, but I can still see that first king jump completely out of the water and feel the throbbing spinning rod with a red on the other end – as Adam handed it to me.

The next year, Jerry Hayenga and Don Hester joined me on the July trip, and after that is wasn't hard to put together a party of eight, which is the number that can comfortably fit into the Gray's basement, walkout apartment on the Kenai.

THE NEXT YEAR

JERRY HAYENGA AND DON HESTER AND I HEAD FOR ALASKA

Jerry, Don and I chose the third week in July, again, so that we could fish both kings and reds, and we were also determined to save one day for halibut. I won't go into detail about our fishing for kings and reds because it was pretty much a repeat of Chad and my experience the previous summer. I will have to confess, however, that Jerry was far more successful in catching reds than I had been. The very first afternoon at Gray's we tried for reds. I had told Jerry and Don more than once on the way to Alaska everything Adam had taught me. Once we were rigged-up, I tried to demonstrate all that I had told them, but to my embarrassment, I never even had one on! After an hour of frustration, I announced that I was going to go up to the apartment and take a nap to rest up from the long trip. Don decided to join me.

*Jerry Hayenga and his
50 pound Halibut.*

Jerry Hayenga (St. Cloud, MN) with his first daily limit of Sockeye Salmon (Reds).

A couple of hours later, I woke up, expecting to find that Jerry had joined us, but Jerry's bed was empty and he was nowhere to be seen. So I walked across the lawn to where I could see over the bank to where we had been fishing, and there he was, trying to net a sockeye! I yelled "Let me help you."

The fish was pretty well worn out and netting it was pretty easy. "Wow", I said, "Is that your first?"

"No, look back in the bushes," Jerry responded.

And I did. To my amazement there were two beautiful reds lying there!

"As you can see," Jerry said, "I've caught my limit." (which was three a piece)

About that time, Don wandered on the scene. In the next half hour or so, Jerry did for Don what Adam had done for me and Chad the previous year. Then, he helped me.

I thought in vain for an excuse for my earlier failure to produce, and finally muttered something about the fish must have just moved in. I really don't know if that is what happened, but it is true that the reds do move up river in schools.

The next day, being Monday, no guided boats were allowed on the river, so Chick had arranged for us to have our day of halibut fishing with a wild but wonderful man named Robbie Carroll on his boat, called "the Irish Lord", named for one of the ugliest fish that swims.

Before dawn, we made the nearly one hour drive down the Homer Highway as far as Ninilchik, and met Robbie there, with his boat on a trailer. We followed him down to the ocean shore, where he unhooked his trailer and invited us to climb a ladder into the boat. In a few minutes a John Deere tractor came along with a hitch on the nose of the vehicle. It hooked onto our trailer and backed us into the water to where it was deep enough for Robbie to lower his two 200 horse outboards and back away from the shore.

An hour later, we were over more than 200 feet of water and Robbie ordered his deck hand to drop anchor. Robbie has a tremendous amount of enthusiasm and he gave us an enthusiastic demonstration of how to fish halibut. He explained that they were bottom feeders and that they loved the remains of a butchered salmon he had woven onto the hook. He added that a lot of weight (in this case we started with three pounds!) was necessary because of the strong current on the ocean floor. He explained that our trip was timed to be during the change of tide. It was much easier fishing during this "slack tide." He proceeded to lower his bait with his thumb on the reel to keep the line from getting tangled. Once the bait hit bottom, he bounced it slowly up and down. Unbelievably, the tip of the thick rod twitched a couple of times. Robbie laughed as he said, "I haven't lost my touch; I've got a bite!"

He let the fish jiggle the rod tip a half dozen times, then set the hook and handed the rod to Don Hester. Fighting the current and the weight and the fish can be a lot of work, but it is a little easier if you reel down until the rod tip is just above the water and then lift it up as far as you can: Reel down, lift up, reel down, lift up – the same technique as we used on the big kings when they were under the boat. About fifteen minutes later, the halibut was on the surface and Robbie gaffed it. He guessed the weight at about 35 pounds and added, "I guess it's a keeper all right; it's a little bigger than a chicken." (which we learned was the name guides gave small halibut. The big ones, over a hundred pounds, are called "barn doors."

Speaking of barn doors, if a halibut is in that hundred pound class or bigger, the guide will harpoon it and then shoot it in the head. Robbie uses a .410 shotgun. Most years we get at least one in that class (but not this trip). Don, Jerry and I each caught two nice fish. Jerry's was the biggest, Robbie guessed it at between 50 and 60 pounds. And that's a lot of good eating!

When we returned to shore, the tractor met us and pulled our boat out of the water. Needless to say, our first halibut trip was a great experience. We try to get in a day of halibut fishing every year. Once in awhile, bad weather will make us postpone the trip until later in the week, but I can't recall a year when we haven't had a successful halibut trip. Some years we have had Robbie's partner, Bill, as our guide, and Bill is about as laid back as Robbie is hyper.

Jerry, Don and I spent the rest of the week with Chick, fishing kings on the Kenai and, in the after hours, fishing reds in front of our apartment. The kings we kept were all nice fish, but nothing huge. Fish over 50 pounds are pretty scarce, but I think all the guys that go up there regularly have topped that weight. Some over 60 pounds, and a couple of us at or near seventy. Of course, that's still a long way from the all time record for kings caught anywhere, and that one was caught on the Kenai – ninety-seven pounds.

Our Halibut guide, Robbie Carroll, helping clean the day's catch.

Jerry Hayenga (St. Cloud, MN) with a 63 pound king salmon.

Gordie Dezell (Staples,MN). His King is almost as big as he is!

Joe Styles (St. Cloud, MN) with a 55 pound King.

Eric Peterson (Rockford, Ill.) with his first King over 50 pounds.

Eric Peterson, two years later, with his second King over 50 pounds.

*Bruce Lund (Staples, MN)
with his first King Salmon.*

*Bruce Lund with his second
King Salmon (the next day).*

Chris Johnson, Joe Styles, Eric Peterson, Greg Johnson, Sam White,
Ken Shorter & Steve White with their limits of Halibut.

The author with his 70 pound King

Kevin Crocker (Big Lake, MN) with a nice Halibut – about 60 pounds.

Ling Cod out of Homer – 2005.
Chris Johnson, Joe Styles & Eric Peterson with their first ever catch of Ling Cod. Fortunately
they taste much better than they look! The smaller red fish are called yellow-eyed rockfish.

Ling Cod out of Homer – 2006
Sam White, Adam Kishbaugh (Kenai Guide), Eric Peterson, Joe Styles, Steve White & Ken Plocher

The author with his "barn door" Halibut

Adam Kishbaugh, normally a guide on the Kenai River, and his yellow-eyed rock fish.

FISHING THE KASILOF RIVER

Fishing the Kasilof is in sharp contrast to fishing the Kenai, especially in July when the sockeye run is on and it seems like every salmon loving Alaskan is there to get his or her share of reds. Every campground along the Kenai fills up and many of the campers "can" their catch right there. July is also a great time to fish kings on the Kenai and boat traffic can get a bit crowded.

In contrast, no outboards are allowed on the Kasilof; all you see is drift boats, and there aren't all that many of them. There are also fewer cabins and homes so it is much more of a wilderness setting and much more quiet. There is a sockeye run on the Kasilof but it is small compared to the Kenai.

Each year we arrange a schedule which makes it possible for each of our gang to have a day on the Kasilof, two fishermen at a time. Since kings are more plentiful on this river, and fish caught here do not count against the Kenai limit of two, the fifth day is reserved for the two men who have either not kept two kings on the Kenai or have caught the smallest fish. It is possible to fish three or even four men in some drift boats, so we do assign a third man that last day if more than two of our guys have had poor luck.

Generally, the kings do not run as large on the Kasilof, but that is changing. Some of the guides think some of the Kenai salmon have gotten lost and migrated up the Kasilof. Good examples of the larger kings are the photos of the fifty pounders Chris Longbella and Sam White, are holding. Ten years ago, twenty pounds was about the max.

The drift boat guides have a tougher job than those running power boats. The fishable part of the river isn't very long and if the guide allowed his boat to drift freely while his fisherman is fighting a big king, he would drift that whole part of the river and the trip would be over! In the case of the big king Chris is holding, the guide worked the boat over to the shore and out of the current.

Each drift boat has an anchor tied to the stern of the boat and most of the fishing is done while anchored. The swift current gives the lures plenty of action. The guide sits in back of the fishermen. When the anchor is up, the guide is continually rowing to slow the boat's progress down stream.

At the start of each trip, one of the fishermen will follow the guide down to where the fishing trip will end and the guide will leave his truck and trailer there. They will then return to where the boat awaits them and leave the fisherman's vehicle there while they are fishing. When the trip is over, the guide will bring the fishermen back to their vehicle. The drift fishing usually begins where the Soldotna-Homer highway crosses the river.

The Kasilof also has an excellent silver salmon run later in the summer.

Dr. Chris Longbella (Chippewa Falls, WI) with one of our biggest ever Kings out of the Kasilof River. It was over 50 pounds.

Greg Johnson (St. Cloud, MN) with three more typical Kasilof Kings.

Sam White and his 50 pound plus King from the Kasilof.

Eric Peterson (Caledonia, IL) with two nice silvers from the Kasilof.

A drift boat. No boats on the Kasilof can have motors. Drift boats are also found on the Kenai along with the outboard driven boats.

That is a "Quick Fish" lure in the Silver Salmon's mouth.

Cleaning a couple of Silver Salmon.

Dr. Dave Freeman (Staples, MN) and son Mason show off their Silvers.

Dan and Mason Freeman show off more Silver Salmon.

SILVER SALMON

Silver salmon are the acrobats of their species. Virtually all salmon like to jump, once hooked, but silvers just jump higher and more frequently. Over the years we have had several silver salmon jump so wildly that they ended up on shore or in a floating bog. We have even had one silver jump right into our boat! The silvers are also great at reversing their direction. Inexperienced salmon fishermen often assume they have lost their fish. I have seen people even lay down their rods in disgust, with a fish still on! Needless to say, fishing silver salmon is just an awful lot of fun.

Silvers run in the Kenai and Kasilof in August and September. Their spawning time will vary from river to river but they always come after the reds are done. Several years we have returned to Alaska in August just to fish silvers. Every other year there is also a simultaneous run of pinks. On the Kenai the pinks run in even numbered years.

Greg Liefermann (Staples, MN) with the biggest Silver Salmon any of our group has ever caught (18 1/2" pounds). This one came from the Kenai River.

Silver salmon are very good to eat, but for me they don't quite measure up to sockeyes. They also smoke well. In the Alaskan fish markets, silvers are priced just a little lower than the reds.

Generally speaking, silver salmon move in schools and are often found in slack water, sometimes near shore where they are most effectively fished by casting shoreward from a boat. In the years when the pinks are in, about five of every six fish you catch will be a pink; the sixth one may be a silver. In the years when there are no pinks, most guided boats anchor above the hot holes and let their lures drift down into the key areas. Spinners and spoons are favorite lures for casting, but when boats are anchored they will often use eggs, Quickfish or Flatfish. When anchored, you might as well put your rod in a holder and relax. Silvers hit so hard they usually hook themselves.

Like other varieties of salmon, the size of the fish will vary from stream to stream. Generally speaking they will run about a third larger than the reds.

PINK SALMON

HUMPIES

The favorite Alaskan salmon are no doubt the kings, sockeyes and silvers, and perhaps in that order. But the pinks, or "humpies" as they are also called because the male grows a big hump on its back during spawning, really aren't all that bad and we keep a lot of them during their run on the Kenai in August in even numbered years. And they do have commercial value. Much of the canned salmon bought in stores are pinks.

Because the huge hump on the males makes cleaning them more difficult (the hump is not good to eat), we keep only females. The females are easy to butcher and are very good smoked. Because they have thinner fillets they smoke-up a little firmer than reds or kings and some people like smoked fish better that way.

We have also found that fresh pink salmon are excellent on the grill or baked or even fried. But, for some reason, freezing pink salmon is disastrous! The meat gets soft, mushy and tasteless.

Because we want to bring home our limits of silvers on our August trips and because kings are illegal to keep on the Kenai at that time and because the reds are long-gone, all the smoked fish we bring home are pinks. We don't freeze the smoked fish until we get home and for some reason, freezing does not adversely effect the eating quality of smoked pinks.

Pink salmon are also a lot of fun to catch. They gather in schools along the shore and are best caught by casting spinners and spoons. We pretty much catch them while casting for silvers. They are more aggressive (or at least more numerous) than the silvers and will far out-number the silvers you will catch, but they do provide a lot of action.

Dr. Joe Styles (St.Cloud) with a "trophy buck" pink Salmon.

TROUT DOLLY VARDEN AND GRAYLING

Nearly all of the trout we have caught in Alaska were taken while on hunting trips, with one mighty big exception, and that was a twelve pound rainbow I caught early one morning on the Kenai while fishing for silver salmon. Even the guide didn't recognize what we had until it was in the net. Occasionally we have caught small rainbows or Dolly Vardens while fishing salmon on the Kenai or the Kasilof, and although we have kept the nicer fish they were nothing to brag about.

There are good trout streams on the Kenai Peninsula; we just haven't fished them. The headwaters of the Kenai River produce rainbows, and nice ones. We just haven't taken the time while salmon fishing to try for them.

On the other hand, we have caught dozens of rainbows, "dollies" and grayling on each and every hunting trip, and even one trophy size cutthroat on the Newhalen River, and no one knows where that came from. Most of these fish supplemented our diet or were released. Several, however, decorate the walls of our fishermen.

The one trip when we had to move camp for lack of caribou or moose the trout kept us from starving. The plane couldn't get in because of the foul weather and our last five meals were trout. There weren't even grayling or northern pike to add a little variety, just rainbows and Dolly Vardens.

Speaking of northern pike, we have caught many of them on our hunting trips in the little lakes on which we camped. None of them topped ten pounds but they were nice fish and very good eating (once we learned how to de-bone them).

Since we hunted the Lake Iliamna and Lake Clark areas, our most successful fishing was on those watersheds, including the Newhalen, Kvijak and Upper and Lower Talaraks. We did catch many trout and grayling however, in the nameless little streams and even in some of the smaller lakes on which we camped.

We fished the Newhalen from shore near where it leaves Lake Clark and by boat below the waterfall where the river nears Lake Iliamna and across from the Iliamna Eskimo village. On my very first trip I learned a lesson about fishing from an anchored boat on a swift moving stream. I had the second-biggest rainbow of my life on my line and didn't know it would be much easier to land if we pulled the anchor so I wouldn't be fighting both the fish and the current. The hook finally tore out of its mouth although we had it almost in the net several times.

My guide, Tyland Vanlier, holding my biggest ever rainbow.

7 pound Cutthroat Trout

6 pound Dolly Varden (the pink dots and white front edges of the fins are more visible in late season.

7 pound Rainbow Trout

*An Upper Talarek Creek Grayling
– our largest.(About 3 pounds)*

Arctic Grayling – Great little fighters and good to eat.

Ptarmigan – totally white in winters with brown patches in summer.

So what do we use for bait? The good news is that Alaskan trout and grayling seem to be always hungry and not very fussy about what they take. Although we have had our best luck on smaller lures like Mepps spinners or smaller spoons. We have been amazed at how trout and even grayling with their relatively small mouths will hit larger lures.

In early years we fished grayling with black gnat flies, but soon learned that they will take much larger baits.

We have had our best luck with spinner baits for rainbows and dollies, but that's probably because those are the lures we most often throw at them. Smaller spoons really seem to work equally well. So far as color is concerned, any color that resembles salmon or trout eggs seems to be preferred. In other words, any variation of orange or red. In the absence of lures of that color we have often tied on blaze orange yarn.

Salmon eggs also work well. Powders or solutions are available in most Alaskan tackle shops that will toughen the eggs overnight and help keep them together. We have found that "borax" is a pretty good substitute.

In our experience, fly rods and spinning tackle work about equally well. I would suggest you use whichever you are used to.

In our experience, rainbows and dollies may be found in most any river or stream in Alaska. Grayling are another matter. Grayling are where you find them! Both grayling and trout may be found in lakes that have streams running in, out or through them.

So far as eating is concerned, we tend to prefer rainbows. Dollies are "ok" but have softer flesh. More than one first-time Alaskan fisherman has discarded dollies when he got home because he thought the soft meat had spoiled.

My Alaskan friends tend to prefer grayling to trout, but I think that is because nearly all Alaskan fish other than grayling and northerns have red meat.

Most of Alaska's larger lakes (like Clark and Iliamna) have lake trout.

Arctic char are relatively scarce in Alaska but they are found in a few lakes and streams. The late Jay Hammond, former governor of Alaska, had a secret, relatively small lake, not too far from his home on Lake Clark, where he caught some trophies.

One year, as we were returning from a hunt, the pilot swung back, low, over a small lake that had a stream running through it. He told us to focus on the mouth of the stream entering the lake. We saw what looked like small logs, about fifty of them, lined up facing the incoming water. "Arctic char!" the pilot announced. (I suspect this was Governor Hammond's secret lake.)

One year, Ed Morey and Don Hester had no need to return to Minnesota immediately, so they decided to do an overnight on this little lake and try to catch some of the char. When they returned to the lake they could see that the fish were still there, but to their disappointment, they would not hit any of the lures they threw at them. About the only thing that happened that made the experience memorable was that there were a lot of ptarmigan in the area. They only had a rifle with them but Ed told Don, "I'll bet I can catch a couple of them for supper with our landing net."

Don encourage him, and Ed proceeded to crawl slowly towards a covey on his hands and knees. He snared a bird on his first try but it took several more attempts before he landed the second one. They both declared the supper worth the effort and told the story over and over to their buddies back home.

Chapter 7

FISHING RECIPES

CREATED OR COLLECTED IN ALASKA

HALIBUT RECIPES

BAKED HALIBUT WITH SOY SAUCE

Ingredients:
- 2 pounds of halibut fillets (if much more than one inch thick, slice lengthwise into two fillets)
- 1 cup soy sauce
- 1/3 cup sugar
- 1 large Vadalia or other sweet onion, sliced
- 1/2 t garlic salt
- Combine soy sauce, sugar and garlic salt and stir in a pan over low heat until sugar dissolves.
- Lightly grease the baking dish or pan.
- Lay fillets in a baking dish or pan in a single layer. Scatter onion slices over fillets. Spread sauce over fillets. Bake in a pre-heated 350° oven for 20 minutes or until fish flakes easily.
- Instead of baking, fillets may be broiled or barbequed.

BAKED HALIBUT IN MILK

- As many fillets as needed for a meal. If fillets are much more than one inch thick, slice each fillet lengthwise into two fillets.
- Lightly grease baking dish or pan. Lay fish in the pan in a single layer.
- Slice a green pepper and a large onion. Scatter slices over fillets.
- Add enough milk to cover the fillets.
- Bake in a pre-heated 350° oven for 35 minutes or until fish flakes easily.

BAKED HALIBUT WITH SHRIMP AND/OR SCALLOPS
Ingredients: Serves 4.
– 1 1/2 pounds halibut fillets (If much more than one inch thick, slice lengthwise into two fillets)
– 1 cup small shelled shrimp
– 1 cup scallops (If just shrimp or just scallops are used, use 2 cups)
– 1 cup soy sauce
– 1 cup vegetable oil
– 1 cup shredded cheese of your choosing (Swiss or Mozzarella work well)
– Combine the soy sauce and vegetable oil
– Lightly grease a baking dish or pan.
– Lay the fillets in the baking dish in a single layer. Scatter the scallops and or shrimp over the halibut. Sprinkle the soy sauce – vegetable oil mixture over the contents of the baking dish.
– Scatter the shredded cheese over – all.
– Bake in a pre-heated 350° oven or 30 minutes or until fish, scallops and shrimp are done.

BAKED HALIBUT STUFFED WITH CRAB MEAT OR SHRIMP
Ingredients: Serves 4.
– 2 pounds halibut fillets sliced lengthwise so that fillets are less than one inch thick.
– 2 cups chopped shrimp (shells and veins removed) or chopped crab meat.
– 1 cup bread crumbs
– 2 T chopped onion
– 1 T minced garlic (optional)
– 2 cups white wine
– 1/2 cup chopped parsley for garnish
– Combine the crab meat or shrimp, onion, garlic, bread crumbs and wine.
– Lightly grease a baking dish or pan. Lay a single layer of fillets in the pan. Top with the mixture. Bake in a pre-heated 350° oven for 35 minutes or until halibut flakes easily. Garnish with chopped parsley.

HALIBUT BAKED WITH MUSHROOMS

Ingredients: Serves 4.

– 2 pounds halibut fillets (slice fillets in two – lengthwise, so that they are less than one inch thick.)

– 2 cups pre-cooked (canned) mushrooms or 4 cups uncooked mushrooms (sliced)

– 4 t olive oil

– 4 t lemon juice

– salt and pepper

– Lightly grease a baking dish or pan. Pre-heat oven to 350°. Lay half the fillets in the dish. Season with salt and pepper. Sprinkle half the olive oil and lemon juice on the fillets. Scatter mushrooms over fillets and top with remaining fillets. Season top fillets with salt and pepper. Sprinkle remaining lemon juice and olive oil over top fillets. Bake for about 25 minutes or until halibut flakes easily.

BAKED HALIBUT WITH SHREDDED COCONUT

Ingredients: Serves 4.

– 2 pounds halibut fillets sliced in two – lengthwise – so that they are less than one inch thick

– 2 cups (heaping) shredded coconut

– salt and pepper

– 4 T lime juice

– Lightly grease a baking dish or pan. Pre-heat the oven to 350°. Lay half the fillets on the bottom of the baking dish or pan. Season with salt and pepper. Sprinkle with half the lime juice. Scatter half of the shredded coconut over the fillets. Lay a second layer of fillets on top of the halibut already in the dish. Season with salt and pepper. Sprinkle with remaining lime juice. Scatter remaining shredded coconut over top layer of fish. Bake for about 25 minutes or until salmon flakes easily.

SALMON-STUFFED HALIBUT

Ingredients: Serves 4.

– 2 pounds halibut fillets one inch or less thick or one inch or more thick sliced lengthwise

– 2 cups cooked, flaked salmon

– 1/3 cup celery, chopped

– 1/4 cup chopped onion

– salt and pepper

– 1/2 cup bread crumbs

– 2 T melted butter

Sauce ingredients:

– 2 T melted butter

– 1 cup white wine

– 1/3 cup half and half

– 2 T flour

– 1/3 paprika

– Lay a single layer of halibut fillets in a lightly greased baking dish or pan. Season with salt and pepper. Combine the celery, onions, salmon, bread crumbs and 2 T melted butter and ladle over fillets. Lay remaining fillets on top and season with salt and pepper. Bake in a pre-heated 350° oven for 25 minutes or until both layers of fish flake easily.

– Meanwhile, prepare the sauce by combining all ingredients and stirring together over medium heat until reduced by one-third. Ladle the sauce over each serving potion of halibut.

OVEN FRIED HALIBUT

Ingredients: Serves 4.

– 2 pounds halibut fillets one inch or less thick (slice in two lengthwise if necessary)

– pepper

– 1 cup crushed, salted soda crackers (use a rolling pin)

– 3 T melted butter

– 3 T grated cheese of your choosing

– Lay halibut fillets in a single layer on a lightly greased cookie sheet. Sprinkle with pepper. Scatter cracker crumbs uniformly over fillets. Sprinkle with melted butter. Sprinkle with grated cheese. Bake, uncovered, in a pre-heated 400° oven for 20 minutes or until halibut flakes easily.

HOT HALIBUT DIP (but not in degrees!)

– 2 pounds halibut, pre-cooked or left-overs, and flaked or chopped.

– 8 oz. cream cheese

– 2 cups light mayonnaise

– 2 medium size cans green chilies

– 1 small can diced jalapeños

– 1/2 t garlic salt

– 1 cup spicy cheese (like Monterey Jack), shredded or cut into bits.

– 1 cup Cheddar cheese, shredded or cut up

– Using a food processor, combine all ingredients except fish until creamy. Using a large spoon, thoroughly combine with the fish. Cover and refrigerate at least two or three hours before serving (the longer the better). Serve with crackers of your choosing; (I prefer Club brand.)

BEER BATTER FOR HALIBUT OR OTHER FISH

Batter for fish to feed six:

– 1 cup stale beer

– 1 egg

– 1 cup complete pancake flour

– 1 t baking powder

– 1/2 t lemon pepper

– 1/2 t garlic salt

– Stir egg into beer. Add other ingredients and stir into a batter. Be sure batter is thick enough to stick to fillets. If too thin, add flour. If too thick, add beer. Slice fillets if necessary so that they are about 1/2 inch thick. Drop into hot oil. Do not let sides touch. Turn over once so that filets are a golden brown on both sides. Dry on paper towel. Serve with white tarter sauce.

HALIBUT OR LING COD INTO LOBSTER

– Cut fish into one inch chunks. Add 2 T sugar and 2 T salt to each gallon of water. Place water in a pot and bring to a hard boil. Then drop fish chunks into the water and let cook for 5 minutes or until chunks come to the surface. Let drain on paper towel.

– Meanwhile, melt 1/4 to 1/2 pound butter slices (depending on how much fish you have) and stir-in 1/2 t garlic salt per quarter pound of butter. Dip chunks of fish into melted butter.

HALIBUT PATTIES

– 2 pounds Halibut fillets, skinned. Serves 6.

– 2 eggs

– salt and pepper

– cooking oil or butter or margarine

– tartar sauce

– lettuce

– onion and tomato slices (one of each per patty)

– hamburger buns

– Run the fillets through a meat grinder, or they may be chopped fine.

– Beat the eggs, lightly, and then stir them thoroughly into the ground halibut.

– Mold into hamburger-size patties, Season with salt and pepper to taste.

– Fry in light oil (or butter or margarine) over medium-high heat, turning once so that the patties are well-browned on both sides.

– Serve on buns with guest's choice of combinations of tartar sauce, lettuce, onion and tomato.

MY FAVORITE HALIBUT RECIPE (works equally well with ling cod)

Ingredients: Serves 4.

– 2 pounds fillets (no more than one inch thick)

– 2 T lime juice (may substitute lemon)

– 1/8 pound butter (1/2 stick) melted

– 3 T chopped onion

– 1/2 cup grated Parmesan cheese

– 4 T mayonnaise

– 1/3 garlic salt

– 1/4 t Tabasco (optional)

– Brush fillets with lime juice - let sit 10 minutes.

– Broil fish 5 minutes on each side or until fish flakes easily.

– Meanwhile, combine remaining ingredients and brush on fillets. Broil a minute or two or until fish turns brown.

HAL-I-BUTS (hors d' oeuvres)

– Cut halibut steaks into chunks approximately one inch by two inches. Wrap each piece with part of a strip of bacon - secure with toothpicks. Broil about five minutes on each side (turning once) or until fish flakes easily.

SALMON RECIPES

MARV'S* THREE ZESTY BAKED SALMON RECIPES

All three of these recipes are for oven baked fillets. Remove the skin from the fillets, wash and pat dry and then cut into serving size pieces. Cuts should not exceed 3/4 inch in thickness. If the salmon is large and the fillets are thicker than this, cut each of the fillets into two fillets with a horizontal cut starting where the fillet starts to get thicker than 3/4 inch. This will give you 4 fillets per fish; cut into serving size pieces.

Use a baking sheet, sprayed or coated with cooking oil. As you place the cuts on the baking sheet, be sure the sides do not touch each other. Pre-heat the oven to 300° and place the tray in the center of the oven. Bake for a total of 20 minutes.

RECIPE NUMBER ONE
– Season the fish with salt, lemon pepper and dill weed (sparingly).
– Spread regular mayonnaise over the fish (about 1 level T per piece).
– Sprinkle very lightly with parsley flakes.

RECIPE NUMBER TWO
– Season cuts with salt, lemon pepper and a trace of sugar.
– Cover each cut with mild salsa sauce.

RECIPE NUMBER THREE
– Season lightly with salt, lemon pepper and dill weed (sparingly).
– Prepare a mixture of 1 stick butter (melted) and 1 T Worcestershire sauce.
– Bake fish for 5 minutes, then baste with the sauce.
– Bake another 10 minutes, and again baste with the sauce from the pan.
– Cook an additional 5 minutes.

*The Late Marvin Campbell, Brainerd, Minnesota - Developed these three recipes while fishing in Alaska.

BROILED FILLETS
– 2 pounds salmon fillets, cut into serving size pieces (leave skin on). Serves 4.
– Season lightly with lemon pepper

BASTING SAUCE
– 1/4 pound butter, melted
– 1 T Worcestershire sauce
– 1/2 t dill weed
– Place fillets, skin side down, on an oiled grill over ignited (gray) coals or gas flame.
– Combine the melted butter, Worcestershire sauce and dill weed. Baste the fish 2 or 3 times while broiling (depends on thickness of fillet).
– Cover while cooking.
– Fish will be done when it flakes easily at the thickest end.

WHOLE SALMON ON THE GRILL WITH CASHEW STUFFING
– 1 salmon, 5 pounds or larger, dressed
– 1/2 cup lime (or lemon) juice
– Lubricate the fish well with the juice, inside and out. Refrigerate 3 to 4 hours (depending on the size of the fish).

Cashew Stuffing
– 2 cups seasoned croutons
– 1 1/2 cups cashews (optional: crush the cashews)
– 1/2 cup celery, diced
– 1/2 large onion, chopped
– 1/2 t nutmeg
– 1/4 pound butter, melted
– 1/2 cup hot water
– 1/2 t garlic salt
– Season the melted butter with the garlic salt. Sauté the onion and celery in the butter until the onions are translucent. Place all of the dry ingredients in a bowl. Pour the butter-onion-celery mixture over the dry ingredients in the bowl. Stir in the hot water and mix thoroughly.
– Stuff and sew-up the trout. Leftover stuffing may be wrapped in foil and also cooked on the grill. (Do not stuff the fish until you are ready to put it on the grill.)
– Lay the stuffed fish on a well oiled grill over ignited (gray) coals or gas flames. Cover and bake until the fish flakes vary easily on the large end of the salmon. Allow about 8 to 10 minutes a pound, depending on the heat.

SAUCES FOR SALMON

ALASKAN BARBECUE SAUCE*

May be used on fillets or whole fish while they are broiling and/or when the fish is served. Designed for salmon but works very well with other fish.

Ingredients for 2 pounds of fillets or steaks:

– 1/2 pound butter

– 1 lg. clove garlic, diced

– 4 T soy sauce

– 2 T mustard

– 1/4 cup catsup

– dash Worcestershire sauce

– Using a double broiler, melt the butter. Stir in all the other ingredients and continue heating for about 20 minutes, stirring occasionally. Brush part of the liquid on the fillets or steaks while they are broiling and serve the balance (hot) with the meal. The above recipe will be sufficient to use with four servings.

*Courtesy Mary Hayenga, St. Cloud, Mn. (Mary admits stealing this one from her Alaskan relatives.)

DILL SAUCE

Ingredients for approximately 4 pounds fillets or a 6 pound baked fish (live weight):

– 2 T minced fresh dill or 1 T dry dill

– 1 T chopped onion

– 2 T butter

– 1 T flour

– 1/2 cup cream

– 1 cup fish stock*

– salt and pepper to taste

– Sauté the onion pieces until clear. Stir in flour and cook for 3 minutes. Stir in all other ingredients, seasoning to taste. Serve hot over fillets, steaks or baked fish.

*See pages 151, 152, and 153 at the end of this chapter.

MARINADE SAUCE FOR BARBEQUED SALMON
Ingredients for 2 pounds of salmon fillets: Remove skin, cut into serving size portions.
– 1 cup cooking oil
– 1 cup soy sauce
– Place the fish in a shallow, flat dish. Combine the soy sauce and cooking oil. Pour over the fish. If the liquid does not cover the fish, add more in equal portions. Let stand one and one-half hours, rotating fish in the liquid every 20 or 30 minutes.
– Broil fillets, brushing on more liquid once or twice and brush the fillets with the liquid one more time when they are served.

SHERRY CREAM SAUCE
Ingredients for about 2 pounds of fish. Serves 4.
– 1 cup chicken broth, heated (milk may be substituted)
– 3 t flour
– 1/8 t pepper
– 1/2 t salt
– 3 T butter
– 1/2 cup heavy cream
– 2 T sherry
– Melt the butter. Remove from heat and stir in flour, salt and pepper. Blend in hot broth. return to heat and cook (stir regularly) until thick. Stir in cream and sherry.
– Serve over sautéed, broiled or baked fish.

SEASONED WINE SAUCE
Serve over poached, baked or broiled fish.
Ingredients for about 2 pounds of fillets. Serves 4
– 2 cups sparkling wine (or champagne)
– 2 cups heavy cream
– 1 1/2 cups fish stock*
– 1 small onion, minced (or chives or green onion)
– 2 T lemon juice
– 1/4 cup chopped parsley
– 1/2 stick butter (1/8 pound)
– Cook the wine and onion in a saucepan over medium heat until the liquid is reduced to about 1/3 cup. Stir in the fish stock and boil about 5 minutes. Add the cream and continue boiling until about 2 cups remain. Reduce heat and add butter one pat at a time. When it is all melted, stir in the parsley and lemon juice.

*See pages 151, 152, and 153 at the end of this chapter.

HOT BASTING SAUCE

Use for basting and serve the balance of the sauce over grilled or baked salmon.

Ingredients for 3 pounds steak or 6 pounds whole salmon. Serves 6.

– 1 T butter, melted

– 1 cup fish stock*

– 1 small onion, chopped

– 2 t minced garlic

– 1 can Italian style tomatoes

– 1 small green or red pepper, chopped

– 1 T chopped basil or other favorite herb

– 1 T parsley, chopped

– 4 drops Tabasco sauce

– Sauté the onion and garlic in the butter. Add all other ingredients. Stir and cook over low heat until about 1/3 of the liquid has evaporated.

*See pages 151, 152, and 153 at the end of this chapter.

MISCELLANEOUS SALMON RECIPES

SALMON SALAD

– 1 1/2 pounds (6 pieces) salmon fillet (skinned). Serves 6.

– 2 cloves garlic, minced

– 3 T lemon juice

– 1/2 cup olive oil

– 1 t salt

– 1 head lettuce, torn into pieces (salad size)

– 1 cup salsa sauce

– 1/4 pound butter (to sauté fish)

– Cut the salmon fillets into 6 serving size pieces. Use fillets from smaller salmon or cut a thick fillet from a larger salmon into 2 fillets (horizontal cut the length of the fillet).

– Prepare marinade by mixing together the garlic, lemon juice, salt and olive oil. Place the fillets in a shallow, flat dish and pour 1/2 of the marinade over the pieces. Refrigerate, covered, about 30 minutes. Discard this marinade.

– Remove the fish and sauté in butter a few minutes on each side until done.

– Arrange the lettuce on 6 salad plates. Lay the fish cuts (hot or cold) on the lettuce. Drizzle the other half of the marinade over the fish and lettuce. Spoon salsa sauce (about 2 T per serving) over the fish.

SMOKED SALMON DIP
1 pound smoked salmon, flaked (if flakes are very large, chop into smaller pieces.)

– 1 cup mayonnaise

– 1/2 t Worcestershire sauce

– 1 clove garlic, minced

– 2 T celery, chopped fine

– 2 T onions, chopped fine

– 1 cup sweet pickle relish

– 2 T pimentos

– 2 T sliced black olives

– Mix thoroughly and refrigerate before serving.

– Serve with crackers.

SALMON AND CUCUMBER SPREAD OR DIP
– 1/2 pound cooked, flaked salmon (chop if flakes are too large).

– 1/2 cup mayonnaise

– 1/2 cup cucumbers, chopped fine

– 1/4 t white pepper

– Mix thoroughly and refrigerate.

CURRIED SALMON DIP
– 1 pound cooked salmon, flaked (and chopped if flakes are large)

– 1 pound yogurt (plain)

– 1/2 cup mayonnaise

– 4 T chives or onion greens chopped fine

– 1 T curry powder

– 2 T chutney

– 1 t white pepper

– Mix thoroughly and refrigerate.

SALMON – DILL SPREAD
– 1/2 pound salmon, pre-cooked and flaked (chopped if flakes are large)

– 1/2 pound cream cheese

– 2 T lemon or lime juice

– 1/2 t white pepper

– dash of salt

– 1 T dill weed

– 3 T mayonnaise

– 3 T sweet relish

– Use as sandwich spread or on small pieces of bread or crackers as an appetizer.

RAINBOW AND DOLLY VARDEN

These recipes will also work well with other varieties of trout.

The smaller trout are so full of flavor they are best prepared with minimal seasonings or use of sauces. Just season lightly, coat with flour or crumbs and sauté in butter. If they are 10 inches or less, fry them whole (but dressed).

The larger trout, one pound and larger, may be enhanced by any of the following treatments:

TROUT AMANDINE
A restaurant favorite: here's how they do it:
– 4 trout fillets or smaller whole trout. Serves 4.

– flour and salt

– 1/2 cup butter

– 1/2 t onion juice

– 1/4 cup blanched, finely slivered almonds

– 1 T lemon juice

– Wash and dry the fish. Dust with salt and flour. Heat half the butter and onion juice in a heavy skillet and cook fish until lightly browned. Remove and place on a hot serving dish. Pour off the grease remaining in the pan and add the rest of the butter. Add the almonds and brown slowly, then add lemon juice and when it foams, pour it over the fish.

POACHED TROUT

1 1/2 pounds dressed trout, cut into 2 inch chunks, serves 4. (Small trout may be dressed and poached whole.)

Poaching Liquid

– 2 cups water

– 1 onion, sliced and separated into rings

– 1 cup celery, cut into 1/2 inch chunks

– 1 stalk dill (or 1/2 t dill seed)

– 1 T salt

– 8 peppercorns

– Place the poaching ingredients in a skillet or pot small enough so that the liquid will completely cover the fish pieces. Bring to a boil, then reduce heat and let simmer 10 minutes. Add the fish; bring to a boil again, then reduce heat and let simmer 6 to 10 minutes or until the fish is done.

GRILLED TROUT WITH HERBS

– 4 1 pound trout (live weight). Serves 4.

– 2 T olive oil

– salt and pepper to taste

– 4 small sprigs dill

– 4 small sprigs rosemary (or other herb)

– 4 bay leaves, broken into 3 or 4 pieces

– Dress the trout but leave whole. Rub outside of fish with the olive oil. Season lightly inside and out. Place 1 sprig of each herb and 3 or 4 pieces of bay leaf in the cavity of each fish.

– Place on a pre-heated, well-oiled grill. Broil about 8 minutes per side, turning once (or until fish is done).

SMOKED WHOLE TROUT

– 4 - 1 pound (live weight) trout. Serves 4.
– 2 double handfuls of hardwood chips
– 2 T olive oil
– 1 t thyme
– 1 t rosemary
– salt and pepper to taste
– Dress the trout and rub them (outsides only) with olive oil.
– Pre-soak the wood chips (30 minutes).
– Season the fish inside and out with salt and pepper.
– When the charcoal is ready (gray in color), throw the wet woodchips onto the charcoal.
– Place the fish, cavity opening down, on a well oiled grill. Cover and cook until the fish flakes easily at the large ends.

MICROWAVE TROUT

– Dress a one pound trout per person. (Leave on head and tail but gut and wash). Rub inside and out with lemon wedge; season lightly with salt and pepper. Lay in baking dish and cover head and thinner part with foil (providing foil may be used in your microwave). Cover with plastic; vent a few places with a fork.
– About six minutes will cook one trout; add about three minutes for each additional fish.
– Garnish with parsley and serve with lemon wedges and/or tartar sauce.

*Shore lunch is always special
– especially when prepared by a guide.*

GREAT SLAVE LAKE GUIDES' RECIPE
FOR LAKE TROUT FOR SHORE LUNCH

– 2 pounds lake trout fillets, skinned, washed and patted dry. Serves 4.

– 1 1/2 cups flour in a heavy-duty paper bag

– 1 t salt

– 1 t pepper

– 2 eggs

– 1 1/2 cups water

– 1/2 cup cooling oil (they usually use a solid shortening)

– Cut trout into serving size portions.

– Thoroughly shake the flour, salt and pepper together in the paper bag.

– Mix the egg and water together in a bowl.

– Shake two or three cuts of fish at a time in the bag with the seasoned flour until well coated.

– Dip into th egg wash and then fry in plenty of oil in an iron skillet over a hot fire – turning once – until golden brown on both sides.

Deboning Northern Pike

Figure 1. *Cut an inverted "V" along the ridge "Y" bones.*

Figure 2. *Lifting the ridge of "Y" bones out of the fillet.*

Figure 3. *Continuing to cut and lift the "Y" bones out of the fillet.*

NORTHERN PIKE

– Many of my Alaskan friends enjoy the white meat of the northern pike as a respite from all the red-meated trout and salmon.

– Long underrated for its culinary qualities because of its difficult bone structure, the northern pike has become more popular in recent years as fishermen have learned to de-bone the fillets. It should also be noted that bones are not a problem when the fish is ground or pickled. Baking, also makes the bones easier to handle.

– The pictures, on the opposite page, show one procedure that works quite well, and even though about 15% of the meat is sacrificed, it is well worth it.

1. Fillet the northern the same as you would a walleye or any other fish. Leave the skin on the fillet until after you have finished the de-boning process.

2. The ridge of meat containing the bones will be visible. Cut an "inverted V" along the sides of this ridge, but not all the way through the fillet, as shown in figure #1

3. Make a horizontal cut between the ends of the "V" at the large end of the fillet. Now lift the ridge of bones in one strip out of the fillet as you release it with your knife. (figures #2 and #3)

4. Run your fingers (carefully) down the cut; if you feel any "Y" bones left - remove them.

5. Skin the fillet.

– Smaller northerns may be deboned – quickly – by cutting off the tail piece (about 1/4 of the fillet) which usually has few bones. Then make your "V cuts" all the way through the fillet. With this process it is better to remove the skin before you make the cuts just described. You will end up with two rather long, narrow fillets or "fish sticks," plus the tail piece.

– If the fillets from a large fish are too thick to fry well (especially if you like your fish crisp), try slicing the fillet in two – lengthwise, with a horizontal cut.

WHOLE NORTHERN BAKED WITH HERBS

– 1 whole northern pike, four pounds live weight or larger, scaled, with head, tail, fins, and entrails removed – washed and dried inside and out. Allow 1/2 pound dressed weight per serving.

– 1/4 pound butter, melted

– 2 T lemon juice

– 6 to 12 sprigs of herbs of your choosing.

– With a four pound (live weight) pike use 6 or 7 sprigs. Add the equivalent of one additional sprig per pound for larger fish. Basil, tarragon, dill, parsley and thyme are all possibilities. If you cannot find fresh herbs, use dried or flaked. If all you can have is the powder or minced very fine – use sparingly.

– Rub the dressed fish inside and out with the lemon juice* and then brush inside and out with the melted butter. Season to taste with salt nd pepper. Add the herbs. Fasten the body cavity closed with wood skewers or use needle and thread. Place the fish in a roasting pan, but lay foil on the bottom first for easier cleaning. If you Bake in a pre-heated 350° oven allowing 10 minutes for each inch of thickness. The last 15 minutes, uncover the roaster or open the foil along the back.

– Check for doneness by trying the large end of the fish with a fork to see if it will flake.

*If time permits refrigerate the northern for 2 or 3 hours after you have rubbed it with lemon juice.

FRIED NORTHERN FILLETS WITH HERB SEASONING

– 2 pounds deboned and skinned northern fillets. Serves 4.

– vegetable oil, butter or margarine

– 1 cup cracker or bread crumbs or one of the commercial coating mixes* available.

– 1 T minced or powdered herbs, such as basil, tarragon, dill or thyme. The total of all spices combined should not exceed 1 1/2 tablespoons and go easy on the tarragon.

– 1/2 t salt

– 1/2 t white pepper

– 1 large egg

– 1 cup water

– Cut the fillets into serving size pieces, wash and pat dry with paper towel.

– In a bowl, thoroughly mix all seasonings and herbs with the crumbs. Beat the egg into the water. Dip each piece of fish into the egg wash and then into the seasoned crumbs.

– Sauté over medium-high heat until the fish is opaque and flakes with a fork.

*If a commercial mix is used, it probably already contains a variety of seasonings. Try a piece of fish with just the mix before you consider adding other spices.

GRILLED NORTHERN KABOBS
– 1 1/2 pounds skinned, deboned northern pike, cut into 2 inch squares
  and seasoned lightly with salt and pepper. Serves 4.
– 1 pound large mushrooms
– 2 green peppers cut into chunks
– 1 zucchini squash, sliced thick
– 8 small tomatoes, (cherry size)

BASTING SAUCE
– 1/4 pound butter, melted
– 1 clove garlic, minced
– 1/2 t Worcestershire sauce
– 1/2 T lemon
– Stir together all ingredients and brush all sides of each chunk of northern pike.
  Also baste the vegetable pieces.

POACHING LIQUID FOR MUSHROOM
– 1/2 cup white wine
– 1/2 cup water
– Combine water and wine; bring to a boil; poach mushrooms 2 or 3 minutes.

BROILING PROCESS
– Place alternately, pieces of fish, mushrooms, green pepper, tomatoes, and
  zucchini on wire skewers.
– Broil over hot coals for about 5 or 6 minutes, turning once, or until fish chunks
  are opaque.

NORTHERN NUGGET HORS D'OEUVRES
WITH SWEET AND SOUR SAUCE
– 1 pound deboned, skinned northern fillet. Cut into 1 inch square pieces.
  Hors d'oeuvres for 4.
– 1/2 cup crumbs (bread, crackers or commercial mix)
– salt and pepper to taste
– cooking oil, butter or margarine
– Season the nuggets, toss them in the crumbs, and sauté them over medium-high
  heat, turning them so that all are brown on all sides. (If the crumbs do not stick to
  the nuggets, beat an egg into a cup of water and dip the fish in the egg wash first.)

SWEET AND SOUR SAUCE

– 3/4 cup sugar

– 1/2 cup rice wine or cider vinegar

– 1/2 cup catsup

– 1/2 cup water

– juice of 1 lemon

– 1 t soy sauce

– 1/4 cup cornstarch dissolved in 1/4 cup water

– Combine sugar, vinegar, catsup, water and lemon juice in a saucepan. Cook over medium heat 3 to 4 minutes. Stir in soy sauce and dissolved cornstarch. Bring to boil, stirring constantly. Cook until thick and clear.

– Serve while both the fish and the sauce are warm. Insert a toothpick into each nugget for easier handling.

CREAMED NORTHERN WITH HORSERADISH SAUCE

– 2 pounds fillets, skinned, deboned and cut into 1 1/2 inch chunks. Serves 4.

– 1 lemon, sliced

– water

– 1 T salt

– Cover the fillet chunks with water, add the lemon slices and salt, and bring to a boil. Fish should flake easily when done (about 15 minutes). Prepare the sauce from the following ingredients:

Sauce:

– 1 cup light cream

– 1/2 cup water in which fish was boiled

– 3 T butter

– 2 T flour

– 2 T grated horseradish

– Melt the butter, stir in the flour, add the fish stock and cream. Place the fish chunks in the sauce and bring to a boil briefly. Remove from heat and stir in the grated horseradish. Serve the fish and the sauce over boiled potatoes. Add a generous pat of cold butter on top of each serving.

FISH SOUP

– 1 1/2 pounds deboned northern or other fish, cut into one-inch cubes. Serves 6.

– 2 cups milk

– 3 cups water

– 1/2 cup celery, chopped

– 1 medium onion, sliced (pick apart the slices)

– 3 large potatoes, diced (bite-size chunks)

– 10 peppercorns

– 1 bay leaf

– 1/2 T salt

– 1/2 stick butter (1/8 pound)

– 1 T flour

– Start with the 3 cups of water in a kettle; add the potatoes and bring to a boil. After boiling for 3 or 4 minutes, add the fish, salt, whole black peppers, onion an celery and continue at a slow boil until potatoes can be easily pierced with a fork.

– Mix the tablespoon of flour into the milk until smooth. Reduce heat to "simmer". Add the flour-milk mixture to the soup and stir until thoroughly blended. Add butter a little at a time and continue heat until butter is melted (about 5 minutes).

POACHED NORTHERN

– 2 pounds northern pike fillets, skinned and deboned, cut into 3-inch pieces.

– 2 quarts water

– 1/2 cup white vinegar (preferably wine vinegar)

– 1 large onion, sliced

– 1 stalk celery, cut into chunks

– 2 T minced parsley

– 12 peppercorns

– 1 bay leaf

– 1 T salt

– Combine all ingredients in a cooking pot, except the fish. Bring to a boil and then reduce heat and let simmer for 1 hour. Add fish pieces and increase heat slightly so that it begins to boil. Fish is done when it is opaque (5 to 10 minutes).

– Serve fish with melted butter. Discard poaching solution and ingredients.

NORTHERN PIKE CHOWDER

– 2 pounds deboned, skinned fillets cut into 1 inch chunks. Serves 6.
– 1 large green pepper, sliced and cut into pieces about 1 inch long
– 1 large onion, sliced and broken into circles
– 1 cup celery, diced, 1/2 inch chunks
– 2 cloves garlic, minced
– 1 - 10 1/2 oz. can tomato soup
– 1 - #2 can stewed tomatoes
– 2 cups tomato juice
– 1 - 14 oz. can evaporated milk
– 1 chicken bouillon cube, crushed
– 1 t tarragon
– 3 bay leaves
– 1/2 t white pepper
– 1/8 pound butter
– Sauté the green pepper, onion, celery and garlic in the butter until the onion is translucent. (4 or 5 minutes).
– Combine all the ingredients in a 3 quart sauce pan (except for the fish) and bring to a boil. Reduce heat and let simmer uncovered – about 15 minutes. Add northern pieces and continue to cook for about 10 minutes or until the fish is opaque.

GROUND NORTHERN PATTIES

– 2 pounds northern fillets, skinned, but need not be deboned. Serves 6.
– 2 eggs
– salt and pepper
– cooking oil or butter or margarine
– tartar sauce
– lettuce
– onion and tomato slices (one of each per patty)
– hamburger buns
– Run the fillets through a meat grinder (fine setting). If the northern has been deboned, it need not be run through a meat grinder. Just chop it fine with a knife. If bones may still be seen in the ground meat, run the fish through the grinder again.

– Beat the eggs, lightly, and then stir them thoroughly into the ground northern.

– Mold into hamburger-size patties. Season with salt and pepper to taste.

– Fry in light oil (or butter or margarine) over medium-high heat, turning once so that the patties are well-browned on both sides.

– Serve on buns with guest's choice of combinations of tartar sauce, lettuce, onion and tomato.

THREE FAVORITE STUFFED NORTHERN PIKE RECIPES

All three recipes call for placing the stuffing between pieces of northern approximately 3" by 6". In each case begin by deboning enough fillets to make twelve pieces of that size. It should be noted that pieces smaller than 3" by 6" can be used to make the top layer of fish, so nothing need be wasted.

For each recipe, lay six pieces of fish in a baking dish and sprinkle with seasoned salt.

RECIPE NUMBER ONE Northern stuffed with vegetables – Serves 6.

– 6 medium carrots

– 3 medium zucchini

– 3 T butter

– 3 cloves garlic, minced

– seasoned salt

– Shred carrots and zucchini; sauté until slightly soft in the butter and minced garlic. Sprinkle with seasoned salt and toss while cooking.

– Place a layer of cooked vegetable mixture over each of the six pieces of fish in the baking dish. Cover with the remaining pieces of fish. Sprinkle top layer with seasoned salt. Bake at 350° about 30 minutes, covered.

– Serve as is or top with hollandaise sauce.

RECIPE NUMBER TWO Northern stuffed with Spinach – Serves 6.

– 2 bunches fresh spinach

– 2 T butter

– 1 clove garlic, minced

– 1/4 cup parmesan cheese

– 3/4 cup sour cream

– 3/4 cup fine breadcrumbs

– Wash spinach and discard stems. Melt butter in large sauce pan or skillet. Add minced garlic. Add spinach, tossing until wilted. Stir in parmesan, sour cream and breadcrumbs.

– Place a layer of spinach mixture on each of the six pieces of northern in the baking dish. Cover with the remaining six pieces. Bake covered for about 30 minutes at 350°.

RECIPE NUMBER THREE Northern Stuffed with Smoked Salmon

– 1 lb. smoked salmon

– 1 - 8 oz. pkg. cream cheese

– 2 T lemon juice

– 2 T horseradish

– seasoned salt

– Soften cream cheese. Add lemon juice, horseradish and flaked smoked salmon. Blend thoroughly. Place a layer of the smoked salmon mixture over each of the six pieces of northern in the baking dish. Top with the remaining pieces of fish.

– If desired, top with mornay sauce before baking.

– Bake covered in a 350° oven for about 30 minutes.

– If sauce is used, remove covering last 10-15 minutes to allow top to brown.

MORNAY SAUCE – Makes 2 cups

– 4 T butter

– 4 T flour

– 1 t seasoned salt

– 1 t nutmeg

– 1 1/2 cups milk

– 1/2 cup dry white wine

– 1/2 cup grated Swiss cheese

– Melt butter; add flour, salt and nutmeg. Cook over low heat until bubbly. Blend in milk and wine. Cook, whisking until thickened. Add cheese and whisk until cheese melts.

LIQUIDS FOR USE IN FISH RECIPES
GIVEN PREVIOUSLY IN THIS BOOK

RECIPE #1 (a French recipe)

Ingredients:

– 2-3 cups of left-over fish

– 3 quarts of water

– 1 large onion, sliced

– 3 stalks celery, chopped

– 2 large carrots, sliced

– 2 bay leaves

– 2 T salt

– 6 peppercorns

– 4 T lemon juice

– 1 T minced herbs of your choosing (such as thyme, dill, tarragon, etc.)

– white wine (optional)

– If wine is used, reduce the water by the number of cups added. No more than half the liquid need be wine.

– Combine all ingredients in a cooking pot. Bring to a boil. Reduce the heat and let simmer - partially covered - for a full hour after the liquid starts to boil. Strain out and discard all skins. The liquid may be frozen for future use.

RECIPE #2 (featuring cucumbers)

Ingredients:

– 2 cups left-over fish

– 2 quarts water

– 2 cups white wine

– 1 large cucumber, sliced

– 1 stalk of dill, broken

– 2 bay leaves

– 12 peppercorns

– 2 T salt

– Combine all ingredients in a cooking pot. Bring to a boil. Reduce heat and let simmer – partially covered - for an hour after it begins to boil. Fish may be added at this time or the solids may be strained out and just the liquid used for poaching. Liquid may be frozen for future use, but strain out the solids first.

COURT BOUILLON
Ingredients:
– 3 quarts water
– 1 T butter
– 1 t salt
– 2 T lemon juice and the sliced rind
– 3 peppercorns
– 1 bay leaf
– 1/4 cup sliced onion
– 1 stalk celery, chopped
– 1 carrot, sliced
– Combine all ingredients. Bring to a boil, reduce heat and simmer for about 30 minutes. Sauce may be strained before using for poaching. The strained liquid may be frozen for future use.

FISH STOCK #1
Prepare fish stock for use in other recipes.
Ingredients:
– fish trimmings, bones, head meat (or the whole head) 2 to 3 pounds
– 2 large onions, sliced
– 3 stalks celery
– 3 bay leaves
– 12 peppercorns
– 1 T mined dill and/or other spices such as tarragon or thyme
– water
– white wine (optional)
– Clean all fish parts. If you use heads, crack them with a hammer. If you choose not to use whole heads, cut out the cheeks and use them.
– Place all ingredients in a cooking pot. Cover with water. (If you use wine, cover with equal parts of water and white wine.) Bring to a boil and then reduce heat; let simmer for about 1 1/2 hours. Skin off any foam or solids that come to the surface as they form. Strain through very fine mesh screen or cloth. Keep the liquid and throw away the solids. The liquid may be frozen for future use.

FISH STOCK #2

Ingredients:
– 2 pounds fish parts (heads, bones, trimmings)
– 1/4 pound butter
– 1 onion, large, sliced and separated into rings
– 4 T minced garlic
– 12 peppercorns
– 2 T thyme, chopped (dried)
– 1 t tarragon
– 6 cups red wine
– Sauté the onion and fish until the onion is clear (about 3-4 minutes). Add 1/3 of the wine. Continue cooking until the meat falls off the fish bones. The wine will be nearly evaporated. Add the rest of the wine and reduce heat so that the liquid will simmer but not boil, for about 1 hour. Strain out and discard all solids. Liquid may be frozen for future use.

CEVICHE RECIPES

RECIPE #1

Ingredients:
– 1 pound de-boned white-meated* fish (like halibut or northern pike with skin removed, chopped into small cubes)
– lime juice - fresh - enough to cover the fish
– 4 T sliced black olives
– 2 T chopped sweet onion
– 2 T chopped green pepper
– 2 T pimentos
– 1 t oregano
– 1 large, diced tomato
– salt and pepper to taste
– Combine all ingredients in a container made of non-reactive material (not metal) and refrigerate 6 to 10 hours, stirring every couple of hours, then serve. May be kept refrigerated up to one week.

*Some friends have used salmon and love it.

RECIPE #2

Ingredients:

- 2 pounds fish with bones and skin removed and chopped into small bite-size cubes
- enough fresh lime juice to cover fish - probably 7 or 8 limes, - when combined with vinegar
- 2 cups white vinegar
- 2 sweet onions, sliced and broken into rings
- 4 bay leaves
- tomato, diced
- 1/2 t Tabasco (more if you like it hot)
- 15 whole peppercorns
- optional: a few hot peppers or jalapeños
- 2 T olive oil
- 1 T salt
- Combine all ingredients in a crock or glass bowl (not metal). refrigerate 24 hours, stirring occasionally. Will keep refrigerated up to one week.

OTHER BOOKS BY DUANE R LUND

A Beginner's Guide to Hunting and Trapping
A Kid's Guidebook to Fishing Secrets
Fishing and Hunting Stories from The Lake of the Woods
Andrew, Youngest Lumberjack
The Youngest Voyageur
White Indian Boy
Gull Lake, Yesterday and Today
Lake of the Woods, Yesterday and Today, Vol. 1
Lake of the Woods, Earliest Accounts, Vol. 2
Lake of the Woods (The Last 50 Years and the Next)
Leech Lake, Yesterday and Today
The North Shore of Lake Superior, Yesterday and Today
Our Historic Boundary Waters
Our Historic Upper Mississippi
Tales of Four Lakes and a River
The Indian Wars
Chief Flatmouth
101 Favorite Freshwater Fish Recipes
101 Favorite Wild Rice Recipes
101 Favorite Mushroom Recipes
150 Ways to Enjoy Potatoes
Early Native American Recipes and Remedies
Camp Cooking, Made Easy and Fun
The Scandinavian Cookbook
Cooking Minnesotan, yoo-betcha!
more than 50 Ways to enjoy Lefse
Entertainment Helpers, Quick and Easy
Gourmet Freshwater Fish Recipes
Nature's Bounty for Your Table
Sauces, Seasonings and Marinades for Fish and Wild Game
The Soup Cookbook
Traditional Holiday Ethnic Recipes - collected all over the world
The Life And Times of Three Powerful OjibwA Chiefs,
Curly Head Hole-In-The-Day the elder, Hole-In-The-Day the younger
Hasty But Tasty
Fruit & Nut Recipes
Europeans In North America Before Columbus

ABOUT THE AUTHOR

- EDUCATOR (Retired, Superintendent of Schools, Staples, Minnesota);

- HISTORIAN (Past Member of Executive Board, Minnesota Historical Society);
Past Member of BWCA and National Wilderness Trails Advisory Committees;

- SENIOR CONSULTANT to the Blandin Foundation

- WILDLIFE ARTIST, OUTDOORSMAN.